Korean Wines & Spirits

& Spirits

Drinks That Warm the Soul

KOREA ESSENTIALS No. 18

Korean Wines & Spirits
Drinks That Warm the Soul

Copyright © 2014 by The Korea Foundation

All Rights Reserved.
No part of this book may be reproduced or utilized in any form or by any means without
the written permission of the publisher.

Published in 2014 by Seoul Selection
B1 Korean Publishers Association Bldg., 6, Samcheong-ro, Jongno-gu, Seoul 03062, Korea
Phone: (82-2) 734-9564
Fax: (82-2) 734-9563
Email: hankinseoul@gmail.com
Website: www.seoulselection.com

ISBN: 978-89-97639-52-6 04080
ISBN: 978-89-91913-70-7 (set)
Printed in the Republic of Korea

Korean Wines & Spirits

Drinks That Warm the Soul

KOREA FOUNDATION
한국국제교류재단

Seoul Selection

CONTENTS

Appendix
Information 95

Delving Deeper

INTRODUCTION

Koreans have been producing—and drinking—alcohol for centuries. Along with song and dance, alcohol has always been an essential part of the Korean *joie de vivre*.

Koreans drink a lot, but they don't drink just to get drunk. Of course, Koreans enjoy alcohol as a means to make merry and build cohesion between family, friends and coworkers. But alcohol's place in Korean culture goes far beyond that. Alcohol has historically also been a medicine and a means to preserve perishable ingredients. It even has a place in the sacred rites of Korea's Confucian society, including the all-important ancestral remembrance rites. Because of the important role alcohol has played in their society, Koreans have developed sophisticated brewing techniques to produce a wide range of alcoholic tipples. These techniques serve both to preserve the health benefits of the medicinal herbs often used as ingredients, and minimize the harm alcohol can do, such as hangovers.

When people think of Korean alcohol, they usually think of *soju* and *makgeolli*, the country's best-known beverages. The world of Korean alcohol is extremely varied, however, with each province producing its very own firewater based on local geographical and climactic conditions. Still, Korean liquors do tend to share several key characteristics.

For starters, Korean alcohol tends to be fermented several times: Some 70 percent of Korean alcoholic beverages are fermented at least twice. And while the basic ingredients—rice, water and yeast—are usually the same, how those ingredients are prepared can yield strikingly different results. Rice, for instance, can be prepared in eight different ways before being turned into alcohol, including as a porridge and a variety of rice cakes. The range of drinks—and according to studies, there are about 130 traditional beverages in Korea—is made all the more diverse by the fact that virtually every household used to brew its own alcohol, either for ceremonial or household use.

Moreover, over 50 percent of traditional Korean alcohols are prepared only in specific seasons. While some drinks need to be brewed at specific temperatures, many require ingredients such as flowers and fruits that are available only at certain times of year. Indeed, Koreans of old would enjoy the beauty of seasonal change by drinking tipples associated specifically with those times of the year.

Finally, Korean alcohol was—and to a large extent, still is—viewed as medicine. It makes use of a dizzying array of medicinal herbs, plants and roots, and is prepared specifically to preserve the beneficial health effects of the individual ingredients. This was especially the case in the Joseon Dynasty, when the development of medicine and the proliferation of medical knowledge allowed families to brew their own medicinal wines.

楓。如신 ᅀ창ㆁ為蝌蚪 ᄆᆨ為楮ㄷ稻 鉏

聲編相隨

而成字韻如即字

聲二ㆆ加去聲相

六終而為ᅙ洪字之八聲與去聲相似。諺之入聲無之類其

點為平聲。而文

ㄹ為筆而其字三字

加一點為去為炬ㄴ字且○

狐皮而用也

諺語諺語ㅎ

蟶ㅿ為入。而以

為上去聲

然ㄱ

旨為入

之類

如ᄉᆞᆷ

My friend, if you have some wine at
home
be sure to invite me
When the flowers at my house
bloom
I will call you
Let's discuss ways of forgetting
the worries of one hundred years.

- Kim Yuk (1580–1658)

Chapter One

HISTORY OF KOREAN TRADITIONAL ALCOHOLIC DRINKS

Alcohol is one of the oldest drinks produced by humans, and every culture has myths associated with its origin. However, because fermentation occurs naturally in any fruit or grain containing sugar, early humans probably discovered these natural intoxicants by accident and, finding them to their liking, began to produce them.

It is believed that early Koreans used grain as the main ingredient for making alcoholic beverages, since agriculture became well-developed early in Korea's history. Early Koreans probably waited for the grain to decay and naturally turn into liquor, chewed the grain so that saliva would hasten its fermentation or soaked it in water to make malt. A number of Korean wines and other alcoholic drinks can be traced back to a period before the rise of the three kingdoms of Silla, Goguryeo and Baekje.

THREE KINGDOMS PERIOD

By the Three Kingdoms Period (1st century B.C.–A.D. 7th century), grain wines fermented with yeast were already quite popular. In fact, it was recorded that wine was such an integral part of life that the people of the ancient states of Ye, Buyeo, Jinhan, Mahan and Goguryeo wined, dined and sang incessantly during seasonal festivals like Dongmaeng, an autumnal celebration of the gods held in Goguryeo.

The people of Goguryeo (37 B.C.–A.D. 668) produced a fine wine known as *chiju*, for which they earned a reputation among the Chinese for their fermentation expertise. Inbon, a wine expert from Baekje, introduced the technique of making grain wine to Japan and attained a status on a par with Bacchus as a god of wine. Although ancient documents indicate that *chiju* and other wines called *nangnangju*, *mion* and *yorye* were consumed at the time, there is no record of how they were made.

Holding a Drinking Bout (Shin Yun-bok, 18th century, Kansong Art Museum) depicts a proprietor handing out liquor to her guests at a *jumak*, or a tavern.

Techniques for producing fermented alcohol with yeast or malt were well established by the late Three Kingdoms Period. The wine-making techniques of Goguryeo were exported to China and led to the creation of Korean wines called *goryeoju* and *gogaju*. In the meantime, *sillaju* and *nangnangju* became the most popular alcoholic drinks in the Silla Kingdom (57 B.C.–A.D. 935). According to legend, King Muyeol (r. 654–661), who unified the Korean Peninsula in the seventh century, ate two meals a day, consuming six bushels of rice, six gallons of wine and 10 pheasants.

Although the names of wines associated with Korea's ancient kingdoms have been found in historical records, no descriptions of their ingredients or fermentation techniques have been found. Various kinds of grain wines originated during the Unified Silla period (668–935), with refined grain wines gaining popularity among the aristocracy. Records show that wines such as these were served during a formal dinner hosted by King Sinmun (r. 681–692) in 683.

Gangneung Danoje festival is a local folk ritual passed down from the ancient days in Gangneung, Gangwon-do, and the festival begins with brewing a liquor offering for God.

GORYEO DYNASTY

The brewing of grain wines was further diversified during the first half of the Goryeo Dynasty (918–1392) to include *makgeolli* and *cheongju*, with the later being made by refining *makgeolli*. *Makgeolli* was also called *takju* (turbid wine), *bakju* (thin wine) or *baekju* (white wine) for its appearance and consistency. Besides *makgeolli* and *cheongju*, a distilled liquor called *soju* was introduced to Korea in 1277 through trade with the Mongols and Yuan Chinese.

Celadon liquor bottle from the Goryeo Dynasty

Soju, which was also known as *hongno*, *giju*, *hwaju* and *aragilju*, the last a name alluding to its Arabian origin, quickly gained such tremendous popularity among the upper class that many squandered their wealth on it. The government became so alarmed that it branded *soju* an extravagant commodity and banned it.

Alcoholic brews began to be made not only through a single fermentation process, for example, by fermenting cooked rice with yeast and water as a one-time process, but also through multiple fermentations by adding a certain amount of cooked rice to the already fermented concoction to enhance the flavor and increase the alcohol content. In addition to *soju*, which was produced using a single distillation process, stronger liquors such as *gamhongno*, which required two distillations, were produced.

Most of the Korean liquors known today can trace the origin of their names back to the Goryeo period. They were made mostly with rice and wheat or rice malt. One of the more memorable names introduced at the time was *ihwaju* (pear blossom wine), a variety of *makgeolli* so named because it was brewed from rice with rice malt that had fermented during the pear blossom season.

It was also during this period that specialty wines emerged that added various herbs or fruits to the grain. Wines were produced and sold by temples, which often functioned as inns at the time. An office was established in the royal palace to produce wines for national ceremonies, including the royal ancestral rites held at the national shrine, which required libations of rice wine.

More brewing and distilling techniques were introduced from Sung and Yuan China, together with many new kinds of liquor during the latter part of the Goryeo Dynasty. *Mayuju* (horse milk wine) became known in Korea thanks to contacts with the Mongols, whereas the grape wines from the Western world arrived through Yuan China. Chinese *sangjonju* and *baekju* were favored by the privileged class.

Two distilling techniques were introduced to Korea. One originated in the Middle East or India and was brought to Korea by the Mongols during the early Goryeo period, while the other, originally a Mongol technique, was introduced to Korea after the Mongols established the Yuan China Dynasty, with which Goryeo came into frequent contact. Both techniques soon became firmly established in Korea. Koreans even developed a new technique combining distillation with grain fermentation to produce *noju*, made from a single distillation, and *hwalloju*, which required multiple distillations. Two major methods of alcohol production, grain fermentation and distillation, were thus established during the Goryeo period.

Joseon Dynasty

During the Joseon Dynasty (1392–1910), most Goryeo-era beverages remained in production, with their production techniques being further refined. Nonglutinous rice was replaced with glutinous rice and multiple brewing came to be favored over single brewing.

The variety of wines increased, and distilled liquors, in particular, improved so much so that they were exported during the reign of

Traditionally, Koreans have used clay jars for storing and fermenting food and liquor.

King Sejong (r. 1418–1450). King Sejong encouraged comparative studies of Korean and Chinese medicinal herbs and included information on the distribution of herbs in the *Geographical Description of the Eight Provinces* (*Paldojiriji*), compiled in 1432. He also promoted the publication of medical works such as *Emergency Prescriptions of Native Medicine* (*Hyangyak Gugeupbang*, 1417) and *Compilation of Native Korean Prescriptions* (*Hyangyak Jipseongbang*, 1433). These books had a great influence on the eating habits of the Korean people and contributed to a scientific approach to the Korean diet. The ingredients for medicine and food were often of the same origin: Medicinal herbs, for example, were used in the making of cakes, porridge and beverages, including alcohol.

All kinds of herbs were used in the making of wine. Besides the famous ginseng wine, a variety of pine wines were made using needles, cones, sap, young branches or pollen from pine trees. A "lying pine wine" was stored for a certain time in a cavity made in a pine log. There was even a variety of bamboo wines made from bamboo oil and the water bamboo leaves were boiled in, which was then stored in the hollow of bamboo stalks. Some wines used a single herb whereas others used a combination of many. In all, over

130 kinds of herbs were used to make more than 60 varieties of herbal wines.

Flowers were also added for fragrance. Wines enhanced with chrysanthemum, azalea, lotus, shepherd's purse, rose, camellia or either plum, cherry or apricot blossom were especially popular. The flowers were usually put in a cloth sack and soaked in a wine jar in a mixture of roughly one gallon of flowers to five gallons of wine.

Wines were also made with fruits such as pomegranates, citrons, mandarin oranges, crab apples, grapes, walnuts and pine nuts.

Various ingredients such as pine cone, bamboo, apricot flower, tangerine and pomegranate are used for brewing traditional liquor.

Family members are offering liquor during ancestral rites.

In a Confucian society in which ancestral spirits were revered with the utmost formality, the making of wine used in ceremonial libations became a regular undertaking in every household. Moreover, a housewife had to keep a generous stock of wines for each season because good wine and good food were indicative of her family's status.

Regional wines thrived during the late Joseon period, as each region's traditional wine-making techniques spread to other parts of the country. It was at this time that wines such as *yaksanchun* of Seoul, *hosanchun* of Jeolla-do, *nosanchun* of Chungcheong-do, *byeokhyangju* of Pyeongan-do and *cheongmyeongju* of the Geumcheon area became popular throughout the country.

A new brewing technique combining distillation and fermentation also emerged during this period. Exemplars of this process included *gwahaju* (summer wine), which is a mixture of *soju* and rice wine, and *songsunju* (pine sprouts wine).

After the opening of Korea's ports to international trade toward the end of the Joseon period, foreign liquors were imported in large quantities and quickly became popular with the upper class.

Deoksan Brewery, built during the Japanese colonial period

JAPANESE COLONIAL PERIOD

Japanese sake and beer were introduced to Korea after the two countries signed the Treaty of Ganghwa in 1876, which opened Korea's ports and made way for Japan's eventual colonization of Korea in 1910. In 1907, when Korea was a protectorate of Japan, the Japanese government enacted a tax on liquor, making it a major source of revenue. Homemade wines were banned and a brewery was designated in each village to produce taxed alcoholic beverages. By 1930 traditional homemade wines had all but disappeared, along with the secrets of brewing that had been passed down from generation to generation. Public breweries, which felt the strain of heavy taxes, made little attempt to improve their products. In particular, no improvements were made to traditional *makgeolli*, the main casualty of the flood of Japanese sake.

POST-LIBERATION PERIOD

After liberation in 1945, the taxation of liquor continued in more or less the same form as during the colonial period, except that molasses was substituted by grains in 1952. Beginning in 1962, sweet potatoes were used mainly to make *soju*. Distilled *soju* was banned in 1965 and was replaced with diluted *soju*. In 1974, Korea began importing tapioca to make alcohol.

In the 1970s, Korean companies began the large-scale production of Western liquors such as grape wine, whiskey, brandy, gin, vodka and rum. Domestic beer production had begun decades earlier, when Japan's Kirin and Sapporo beer-makers established breweries in Korea in 1934.

Meanwhile, the quality of traditional wines deteriorated due to a prohibition on the use of rice for making wine. Wines had to be made with flour and other materials because of a chronic shortage of rice, Korea's main staple, which was largely imported. The ban on rice wine was lifted in 1971, and the production of rice

After liberation, various liquors including *soju* and beer were produced in Korea.

Makgeolli delivery man in the 1970s.

makgeolli recommenced soon afterward.

As Korea prepared to host the 1986 Asian Games and 1988 Seoul Olympics, the government began a push to promote Korea's centuries-old brewing culture to visiting foreigners. A survey was taken of culturally significant brews, including lesser-known drinks and home-brewed moonshine. In 1985, the government designated 13 varieties of traditional wine as intangible cultural heritages, including Seoul's *munbaeju*, Chungcheongnam-do's *dugyeonju* and Gyeongju's *beopju*. The makers of these wines were designated human cultural properties. Of these 13 wines, 10 were recognized as city-/province-designated cultural heritages, including Andong *soju*, Jindo *hongju*, Gimcheon *gwahaju*, Jeonju *igangju*, Seoul *samhaeju*, Gimje *songsunju* and Hansan *sogokju*. In 1994, the Ministry of Agriculture and Fisheries designated experts in the making of another four traditional wines—Songhwa *baegilju*, Geumsan *insamju*, Gangwon-do *okhyangju* and Gyeryong *baegilju*—as "masters of traditional wine," providing them with funds to pass on their skills and establish breweries.

Jindo *hongju*, an intangible cultural heritage of Jeollanam-do, is brewed with a traditional method.

Jumak: A Haven for Travelers

Samgang Jumak in Yecheon, Gyeongsangbuk-do, was a place where travelers in the Joseon Dynasty rested before crossing Mungyeongsaejae Pass.

Before the advent of modern industrial society, the *jumak*, or tavern, was a haven for travelers. Its proprietor, invariably a woman, was always happy to serve wayfarers wine, snacks and meals, and engage them in conversation. She was a most welcome sight for travelers.

Jumak were concentrated in and around the Seoul area. There were also many *jumak* at Mungyeongsaejae, the highest pass along the road from the southeast region of Gyeongsang-do to Seoul. Itinerant merchants and scholars coming to Seoul to sit national government exams were just some of the travelers to pass through the area's villages. Jungnyeong, the mountain pass weaving through the Sobaeksanmaek Mountains, and Cheonan Samgeori, a three-pronged fork in Cheonan, Chungcheongnam-do, were other places famous for *jumak*.

Unfortunately, *jumak* began to disappear in the 20th century due to the tax imposed on alcohol by the Japanese colonial regime.

Scenes of Jumak

As *jumak* were located in places bustling with travelers, they were always crowded, particularly at night. Isabella Bird Bishop, a British author and traveler who visited Korea in the late 19th century, had the following to say in her book *Korea and Her Neighbors*.

> There are regular and irregular inns in Korea. The irregular inn differs in nothing from the ordinary hovel of the village roadway, unless it can boast of a yard with troughs, and can provide entertainment for beast as well as for man. Low lattice doors filled with torn and dirty paper give access to a room, the mud floor of which is concealed by reed mats, usually dilapidated, sprinkled with wooden blocks which serve as pillows. Into this room are crowded *mabu* [grooms], travelers, and servants.

Yet, *jumak* were renowned for the generosity of the proprietors and they were often noisy with travelers' chatter. As Mrs. Bishop wrote, ". . . Many a hearty meal and good sound sleep may be enjoyed under such apparently unpropitious circumstances. . . . The Korean inn is not noisy unless wine is flowing freely, and even then the noise subsides early. The fighting of the ponies, and the shouts and execrations with which the *mabu* pacify them, are the chief disturbances till daylight comes and the wayfarers move on. Traveling after dark is contrary to Korean custom."

Jumak (Kim Hong-do, 18th century, National Museum of Korea)

The Makeup of Jumak

In big towns, *jumak* were located near the market area or in clusters along the roads; in small towns or in the countryside, a *jumak* usually stood by itself at the foot of a hill or at a ferry crossing. They did not have gaudy signs like today's establishments, only a kerosene lantern with the Chinese character for wine hanging over their entrance, or simply the word "tavern" in Chinese characters on the door. One could also recognize a *jumak* by the sliced boiled beef or the pork head displayed on a board outside the door, or by a cylindrical bamboo sieve used for filtering wine that was usually hung from the thatched roof.

In the yard were wooden platforms where guests sat while drinking and eating; several sleeping rooms were nearby. The unique feature of *jumak* was that the kitchen was accessible from the proprietor's room, and if she was busy, she could cook while sitting in her own room. In the kitchen, a huge soup cauldron was always boiling, ready for guests at any time of day. In winter, wine bowls were heated by dipping them into the soup cauldron, and boiling water was always kept ready in a small cauldron in a corner. When an order was placed, the wine bowls were filled and heated.

A *jumak* in the isolated countryside had to provide all these standard

Tourists experience a Korean traditional tavern.

services to make lonely and tired travelers feel at home. The most important functions of a *jumak* were to provide drinks, meals and accommodations. The *jumak* was a mixture of today's bar, eatery and inn, as well as a place to exchange news and gossip. And since there were no theaters, tea rooms or karaoke establishments like today, people gathered there to enjoy simple forms of entertainment. It was a haven for weary travelers, but also a place where people interacted and learned of cultural mores among all different walks of life.

Janggukbab, one of the most popular menu items in *jumak*

Jumak generally stocked a limited variety of wine, mostly *makgeolli*, thick, milky rice wine; *soju*, a distilled spirit; and some special homemade wine reserved for wealthy guests. The most popular, especially among commoners, was *makgeolli*. A regular or generous guest was served the dense, hearty variety, whereas a stranger or an unwelcome guest was given wine diluted with water. It all depended on the proprietor's whim.

An order of wine was always accompanied by some food. As each guest entered the *jumak*, he would take a set of chopsticks from a bunch stacked in a container and help himself to the prepared food or put some meat on a charcoal grill.

Jumak also offered meals, the most popular being *janggukbap*. This soup was made by boiling beef brisket, favored for being less greasy, and flavoring it with soy sauce, which gave it a light brown, appetizing appearance. Another delicious dish was an assortment of boiled beef parts—brisket, ox head slices, tongue, liver and oxtail—eaten with a dip of soy or spicy red pepper sauce with a dash of vinegar. It was the perfect complement to a bowl of *makgeolli*.

Although the *jumak* of old have all but disappeared, thoughts of them still evoke feelings of nostalgia in most Koreans.

2
Chapter Two

RICE WINE OF THE MASSES: MAKGEOLLI

*M*akgeolli is one of Korea's oldest and most popular alcoholic beverages. It is usually refered to as *nongju*, or "farmer's wine," owing to its traditional popularity among Korea's farmers, who would consume bowls of the beverage to recover from the aches and pains of agricultural drudgery. Farmers, however, are not the only ones who enjoy it.

During the Goryeo Dynasty, it was called ihwaju, meaning pear blossom wine, because the *nuruk* (a starter that consists of enzyme-carrying mold that has been bred in grain) was made during the pear blossoming season. It was also known as *takju*, or turbid wine, because the thick liquid which resulted from the fermentation of the *nuruk*, water and steamed rice was not filtered prior to bottling. One popular form of *makgeolli* is called *dongdongju*, or "floating wine"; its name derives from the unstrained grains of rice that float on its surface.

This milky wine has a rather low alcohol content of between 6 and 8 percent, with a sour yet refreshing taste caused by it still being in the process of fermenting. The ongoing fermentation also ensures the drink contains a fair amount of carbon dioxide, which adds to its thirst-quenching properties. Partly for these reasons, *makgeolli* was an important part of Korean life, enjoyed during relaxation after a day's hard work, or for celebration or solace on special occasions such as weddings and funerals.

Makgeolli contains a good amount of rice protein (19 percent) as well as vitamins B1, B2 and other B complexes such as inositol and choline. It has about 0.8 percent organic acid, which contributes to its sour taste and thirst-quenching properties, while also promoting a faster metabolism.

BREWING MAKGEOLLI

Makgeolli takes its name from *mak*, which in Korean means "roughly," and *georeu*, which means "to strain or sift." It's a pretty apt description. *Makgeolli* is made from fermented grains strained only very roughly, producing a cloudy, opaque liquid. For this reason, *makgeolli* is also sometimes called *takju*, or "opaque wine." When *takju* is strained to become a clear liquid, it is called *cheongju*. Finally, when *cheongju* is distilled, it becomes *soju*.

As befitting a drink for mass consumption, the *makgeolli* brewing process is not especially difficult. All you need is nonglutinous rice, *nuruk* and water. First, the rice is washed well and soaked for few hours. When the rice is nice and soft, water is drained from the rice and the rice is cooked in a steamer lined with a cheesecloth. This process turns the rice into *godubab*, which is rice fully cooked for brewing. The rice is then placed in a jar of water. Then the *nuruk* is added to the mix, and the jar is placed in a warm place to ferment. This mixture, in turn, is left to ferment for a week in temperatures of 20 to 25 degrees Celsius. During this time the mixture should be stirred at least once a day. As the mix ferments, it will grow increasingly bubbly with a pleasing aroma, while emitting a distinctive crackling sound. When fermentation is complete, the mixture will have separated into a clear liquid on top and a cloudy liquid on the bottom. The clear part of the liquid is then scooped out and this becomes *cheongju*. The cloudy liquid, on the other hand, is filtered out and this becomes *makgeolli*. At this point, water is added to the *makgeolli* and it's bottled. If you're making *makgeolli* at home, you can also add various types of flavoring to the mix, such as honey, sugar or fruit syrup.

Makgeolli is easy enough to make at home, and indeed, this was the way most *makgeolli* was produced until modern times. These days, however, most *makgeolli* is produced in purpose-built

Ripe *makgeolli* is being filtered through a sieve.

breweries. Several of these breweries, such as Sewang Brewery (originally Deoksan Brewery) in Jincheon and Jipyeong Brewery in Gapyeong, date back to the early 20th century and have been designated as cultural properties by the government.

Exploring the Korean Historic Breweries

Jipyeong Brewery

With production methods that have remained relatively unchanged over time, *makgeolli* breweries largely share a similar layout. The first step in brewing is cooking the grains—typically just rice, but sometimes a mixture of wheat or other grains—meaning a space is needed that is well ventilated and can withstand steam. Once the cooked rice has been cooled and dried, it is placed into large jars, often the *hangari*, or Korean clay jars, followed by powdered *nuruk* and water. The *hangari* are placed in a climate-controlled room with thick walls to ferment. The thick walls ensure that the room retains all heat and humidity, with as little variance in temperature as possible. In this space, the *nuruk* can begin assisting the grains as they start breaking down.

Located in the small, rural village of Jipyeong in the county of Yangpyeong in Gyeonggi-do, Jipyeong Brewery is Korea's oldest functioning brewery. Built in 1925, the brewery was acquired by Kim Gyo-seop 60 years ago and has remained in his family ever since. It is currently run by his grandson, Kim Gi-gwan, who quit his job at a public relations firm to take over the family business.

Rather than simply occupying a space that was repurposed for alcohol production, which is common, Jipyeong Brewery was purpose-built, with high ceilings and open second-floor windows specifically designed to keep the place well ventilated. To help maintain a constant temperature, the structure's walls and ceiling have been insulated with rice straw, a feature seen in other historic breweries as well. The wooden construction, too, adds to the excellent airflow.

Unlike many of the older breweries built during the Japanese colonial era, Jipyeong Brewery was not built in a purely Japanese style. Rather, it has grafted Japanese wooden construction onto a Korean base, producing a rather eclectic structure that incorporates many of the features of a *hanok*, or a Korean traditional home.

Another historic brewery established during Japanese occupation is the Sewang Brewery (previously Deoksan Brewery) in Jincheon, Chungcheong-buk-do. Sewang Brewery was founded in 1929 by brewmaster Lee Jang-beom, and has changed remarkably little since then. The beautiful wooden brewery building, designed by a Japanese architect and constructed by Korean builders, was completed in 1930. Built of fir and cedar transported all the way from Mt. Baekdusan, the factory has managed to make it through the decades virtually in its original condition. Until recently, the factory produced high-quality *makgeolli* and *cheongju* using old-fashioned techniques handed down over three generations. Operations have moved to Cheongju, however, and the old brewery is closed for the time being.This is a culturally significant place where architecture, history, cultural tradition and the fine rice and water of Jincheon-gun blend into one.

Sewang Brewery

HISTORY OF MAKGEOLLI

Old *makgeolli* advertisement that says, "A nutritious side dish for labors."

While we don't have any definitive records of when *makgeolli* production began, the 13th century Korean history text *Samgukyusa* suggests that a *takju*-like wine was used in the memorial ceremonies for King Suro of the Gaya Kingdom. It's not until the Goryeo era, however, that much more detailed records of *makgeolli* production begin to appear. In the *Goryeo Dogyeong*, a description of Korea written by an envoy from Song Dynasty China, there is a description of a cloudy, lightly alcoholic drink favored by the common people. Records to *makgeolli*, or *ihwaju* as it was often called back then, can be found in other period texts as well.

In the Joseon Dynasty, homebrewing really took off with the development of and proliferation of brewing equipment. The *Imwongyeongjeji* (*Administration of Our Daily Life in Woods and Fields*), an encyclopedia compiled by scholar Seo Yu-gu in the 19th century, arranged 170 types of Korean liquors into 11 categories. One of these categories was *takju*, into which *ihwaju*, *jipseonghyang*, *chumoju* and *baengnyoju* were placed.

The Japanese colonial era is generally regarded as a dark time for Korean brewing culture. With the authorities placing a tax on alcohol production in 1909 and 1916, unlicensed production of alcohol was banned. *Makgeolli*, however, managed to survive relatively well due to the simplicity of its production—unlike *soju*, which requires a distiller, no special equipment was needed to make *makgeolli*.

Things improved with the end of Japanese colonial rule in 1945, but Korea's difficult economic situation, especially after the devastation of the Korean War, spelled crisis for the brewing industry as ingredients became tough to source. In 1965, the government banned the use of rice to make alcohol, so *makgeolli* makers switched to using imported flour as their chief ingredient. The result was a very different product in terms of taste and color, but it proved popular nonetheless. So popular it was, in fact, that it dominated the local alcohol market throughout the 1960s and 1970s.

As brewers scrambled to keep up with soaring demand, however, they began producing inferior products that were either less mature or artificially fermented, and consumers responded by looking elsewhere. In the 1990s, brewers were once again allowed to use rice as an ingredient, and *makgeolli* producers were quick to adjust. However, the tendency among makers to use cheap, old rice or rice mixed with flour put off consumers. In recent decades, though, *makgeolli* has regained much of its previous popularity as its low alcohol content, lactic acid and rich protein capture the attention of younger, more health-conscious consumers.

Pocheon's Sansawon, a brewery that makes *makgeolli* with pure rice

MAKGEOLLI: IT'S GOOD FOR YOU

Koreans have long known that *makgeolli*, if drunk in moderation, can be good for you. Ancients propagated the drink's therapeutic effects, with the *Donguibogam*, a Joseon Dynasty medical manual, saying that it was used to treat extravasation. *Makgeolli* is 80 percent water, 6-8 percent alcohol, 2 percent protein, 0.8 percent carbohydrates and 0.1 percent fat. The remainder comprises dietary fiber, vitamins B and C, lactic acid and yeast.

Makgeolli is a fermented drink that is rich in lactic acid indeed, it has 500 times the amount of lactic acid in yogurt. *Saeng* (draft) *makgeolli* is especially rich in the substance. Lactic acid boosts your immune system by promoting the growth of healthy micro-flora in your gastrointestinal tract. It also helps prevent constipation and promotes weight loss. The organic acid helps fight off fatigue and promotes blood circulation, too.

Makgeolli has seven of eight essential amino acids, which help prevent high blood pressure and fight off obesity. In addition, a liter of *makgeolli* yields no fewer than 19 g of protein.

A 2011 study by Seoul Sungkyunkwan University found that 3T3-L1 cells (a key source of fat) treated in *makgeolli* extract produced fewer fat cells. This, it is believed, is thanks to the fungus used in the *nuruk* and the drink's high levels of lactic acid.

Even when its sell-by date has expired, *makgeolli* can still work wonders by serving as an ingredient in ecologically friendly fertilizer.

Makgeolli can also be used to make a healthy vinegar and even has cosmetic benefits: Its amino acids promote skin elasticity, while its vitamins B2 and B6 promote skin regeneration and brightning. Its vitamin C, meanwhile, is a good antioxidant, which helps fight aging.

THE MAKGEOLLI SUCCESS STORY

As mentioned above, *makgeolli* has experienced ups and downs over the last century. Speaking to writer Andrew Salmon in *The Wall Street Journal*, Heo Shi-myung of the Sool School in central Seoul explains that *makgeolli*, which in the 1960s accounted for 80 percent of Korea's alcohol market, accounted for just 4 percent by 2009 due to poor quality and changing consumer tastes. By 2011, however, it had climbed back to 11 percent, powered by a *makgeolli* revival among younger Koreans. "Consumption and exports of *makgeolli* are soaring as *makgeolli*'s quality improves, and the number of *makgeolli* brands made of 100-percent homegrown rice increases," explained a Korean tax official to the *Dong-A Ilbo* newspaper. "A high interest in wellbeing among Koreans and the popularity of Korean pop culture in Japan have also contributed to its increasing popularity."

Like the revival of Pabst Blue Ribbon, the *makgeolli* renaissance has been driven largely by younger consumers. This can be seen in the *makgeolli* bars themselves. Once relegated to back alley dive bars, high-end *makgeolli* is now served at chic new establishments opened by Korea's increasingly globalized youth. One venue in the upscale Cheongdam-dong district not only looks like a high-end wine bar but also serves premium *makgeolli* for KRW 12,000 a bottle, a price unimaginable just a few years ago. Even foreigners have gotten in on the act. Taru Salminen, a Finnish expatriate and TV personality, opened her very own *makgeolli* bar in Seoul's youthful

Various fusion *makgeollis* appeal to the palate of young people and women

Hongdae district in 2010.

The drink itself is beginning to change as well. As the consumer base grows younger, brewers are experimenting with new forms of *makgeolli* to attract more sophisticated drinkers. Not so long ago, *makgeolli* used to come in one flavor, but now, flavored *makgeollis* infused with the tastes of a range of fruits and herbs are on offer. Yoon Jin-won, the head of the Korea Liquor Culture Institute, "invented" flavored *makgeolli* in 2005 by adding fresh fruits to the existing *makgeolli* base. The result proved especially popular with female drinkers who enjoy the sweet, fruity taste. More enterprising bartenders, however, are crafting *makgeolli*-based cocktails. Some bars, for instance, even serve a *makgeolli* and champagne cocktail.

Exports of *makgeolli* have been impressive as well, especially to

Japan, where Korean cuisine and pop culture have been all the rage. In 2011, Korean *makgeolli* exports totaled USD 52.76 million, with USD 48.42 million of that going to Japan. To put this into perspective, this was three times the amount of Japanese sake exported to Korea. As was the case in Korea, Japanese demand for *makgeolli* was largely driven by a belief in its healthful properties.

WELL-KNOWN REGIONAL MAKGEOLLI

Pocheon Idong Makgeolli

The mountains and valleys of Pocheon have long been known for their pure waters. Idong Makgeolli, one of Korea's most famous *makgeolli* brands, is a lovely harmony of sweet, bitter and acidic flavors. It goes down very smoothly, too. Even when the popularity of *makgeolli* dwindled in Korea, Idong Makgeolli was a success in Japan after being exported there. A marketing tactic emphasizing its sweet taste, along with a longer shelf life made possible with the development of sterilized *makgeolli* in 1996, made the drink a hit in Japan.

Seoul Jangsu Makgeolli

Seoul's best known *makgeolli* brand is produced at seven breweries throughout the city. It has a balanced flavor combining the sour, sweet and bitter tastes, and is very fizzy. Its alcohol content is around 6 percent.

Busan Geumjeongsanseong Makgeolli

Named for the mountain fortress in the hills north of the city, this is the only *makgeolli* brand in the country to have received government recognition as a "folk beverage." During the Joseon era, residents in the area made a living through producing the local *makgeolli*. By the time of King Sukjong's reign, the Geumjeongsanseong Fortress was being built; this lured in more people from outside the area, who subsequently helped make the *makgeolli* popular nationwide. It even managed to prosper during the Japanese colonial era, being sold in Japan and Manchuria. This *makgeolli* is made using *nuruk* prepared in the traditional way.

Gangwon-do Gangnaengi Yeotsul

Mountainous Gangwon-do is famous for its corn, so it's little surprise that local farmers learned to make booze from it. Among *gangnaengi yeotsul* made in Gangwon-do, the one from the Chuncheon region is the most famous. Made from corn mixed with malt, *gangnaengi yeotsul* has both a savory, corn flavor and the sweetness of malt.

Anyang Ongmiju

A specialty of the Gyeonggi-do town of Anyang, this take on *makgeolli* uses brown rice, corn, sweet potato, yeast and malt to produce a drink that not only tastes good, but also has numerous reported health benefits. Anyang *ongmiju* is thought to be good for the skin and to help prevent arteriosclerosis. A well-made bottle of *ongmiju* has a beautiful lemon-yellow color. Also, compared to other alcoholic drinks, the tipsy feeling after drinking comes on slower, and hangovers are fairly minimal.

Jeju Omegisul

Korea's largest island, Jejudo is essentially a gigantic volcano, with volcanic soil that isn't suited to the cultivation of rice. Millet is an excellent substitute, however, so islanders brew a unique local alcohol, *omegisul*, made from crushed millet cakes. The cakes are boiled, crushed and fermented with *nuruk* and water. After a week, the clear liquid at the top is skimmed off for use in ancestral rites ceremonies, while the muddier layer to the bottom is sieved and served as *omegisul*. Like its mainland cousin, *makgeolli*, *omegisul* was typically drunk by farmers working in the fields. It has a sweet, almost honey-like flavor.

The Genial Makgeolli Street of Jeonju

The city of Jeonju, the capital of Jeollabuk-do, is not only famous for its *hanok* (Korean traditional house) village but also for its unique and varied food culture. In fact, the area was even designated a City of Gastronomy by UNESCO in 2012. Jeonju's most well-known dishes include *bibimbap*, a mixed vegetable and rice dish popular with foreigners; *hanjeongsik*, a full-course Korean meal with various side dishes; and *kongnamul gukbap* (soybean sprout soup with rice), known to be a good remedy for hangovers. Jeonju is also known for its alcohol production, namely, its *igangju* and *makgeolli*. The former has been popular since the olden days, as it was one of the Joseon era's three most renowned alcoholic beverages, along with Pyeongyang's gamhongno and Jeongeup's *jungnyeokgo*. Part of what makes Jeonju ideal for Korean spirit making is its clear, pure water, as well as the availability of high quality rice from Korea's biggest rice producing region, the Honam Plains.

It is Jeonju's *makgeolli*, however, that has become a staple in modern times. The cluster of *makgeolli* joints that make up Jeonju's "*makgeolli* street" is a popular destination for those seeking a bowl of traditional rice wine and free *anju* (side dishes served with alcoholic beverages). At any one of these establishments, a full kettle of *makgeolli* costs a mere KRW 20,000, and arrives with around 20 different *anju* dishes including savory pancakes, fish, oysters, vegetables and boiled beef or pork slices. Also, with each extra kettle, more expensive *anju*, including *hongeo samhap* (fermented skate and steamed pork slices served with kimchi), *bulgogi* (barbecued beef), *sannakji* (sliced raw octopus), *ganjang gejang* (soy sauce-marinated crab) and *yukhoe* (Korean-style raw beef) are served. For those curious about trying new types of *anju*, the only thing to do is to call out for one more kettle.

Jeonju's *makgeolli* street became famous during the late 1990s amid the Asian financial crisis, a time when people started gathering in these restaurants looking to drink away their financial woes. Restaurant owners say that, back in those days, when customers finished the *anju* on their table, the owners would refill the dishes for free, feeling empathetic to their situations. This is how the *anju* system seen in these restaurants first began. The street became known as a genial, warm-hearted space, somewhere that locals could go to fill their empty bellies and lift their spirits. Nowadays, the street has become popular with not only locals but visitors as well, leading to one- or two-hour wait times to get a seat on weekends.

There are eight *makgeolli* streets in Jeonju, including the original one in Samcheon-dong and newer areas in Seosin-dong, Gyeongwon-dong and Hyoja-dong. With over 30 *makgeolli* restaurants, Samcheon-dong is the most popular with visitors, while the Seosin-dong street is more popular with young people. If you would like to pass through the *hanok* village before arriving at a makgeolli street, you would be best advised to go to the Gyeongwon-dong area. The *makgeolli* streets in Hyoja-dong, Pyeonghwa-dong and Ua-dong don't have quite as many options as the others but tend to attract more locals. Each street has its unique charm, and it can be fun to pick and choose between each restaurant's specialty menus.

If you are interested not only in drinking alcohol but also in the process of making alcohol, it is worthwhile to visit the Jeonju Traditional Wine Museum and the brewery located inside the *hanok* village.

3

Chapter Three

THE WORLD'S BEST-SELLING DISTILLED LIQUOR: SOJU

The liquor that appears at meals, picnics, and practically any other gathering, even in travel bags, is a green-bottled phenomenon that Koreans savor above all others. Just what is *soju* all about?

In 2012, Koreans drank 3.4 billion bottles (360 mL) of *soju*. This comes to an annual average of 88.4 bottles per adult, or 7.4 bottles per month. Considering that these figures also include non-drinkers and occasional imbibers, it is clear that many Koreans consume an incredible amount of *soju*. According to a recent survey held in Korea, 65 percent of respondents thought of *soju* first when alcohol was mentioned. It is no exaggeration to call *soju* the national drink of Korea.

FROM ARABIAN LIQUOR TO KOREA'S FIREWATER OF THE MASSES

Soju's history is colorful as well as tumultuous. It is not indigenous to Korea, but was introduced to the country by invaders. In the early 13th century, when the Goryeo Dynasty ruled the peninsula, the Mongol invaders brought with them a strong distilled liquor, the likes of which Koreans had never encountered. This became the drink we now know as *soju*. At the time, Koreans enjoyed fermented tipples such as *cheongju* (refined rice wine) and *makgeolli* (unrefined rice wine).

Soju was known in Mongol as *araki*, from the Arabic term *araq*, which refers to distilled liquor. Thus *soju* was originally developed in Arabia and passed through Mongolia and Manchuria before arriving in Korea. According to one account, Genghis Khan introduced the Arabian *araq* to Mongolia after his invasion of the Khwarezmian Empire, which his grandson Kublai Khan, the first emperor of the Yuan Dynasty, then brought to Korea on his way to invade Japan. It could be said, then, that *soju* was spread through war. The fact that the sites of former Mongol base camps, such as Gaeseong, Andong and Jeju Island, are now famous *soju*-producing regions offers compelling support for this historical account.

After the Mongols left, their liquor gained wide popularity among the upper crust of Goryeo society. *Soju* was made from grain, then a precious commodity, which limited its availability to the privileged classes. Among them, however, it gained such popularity that *Goryeosa* (*The History of*

Pottery for distilling fermented liquor

Goryeo) records an edict issued by King U (r. 1374–1388) in 1375: "The people know nothing of austerity, but squander their fortunes on *soju* and silk and dishes of gold and jade, so henceforth these things shall be strictly forbidden." This royal decree had little effect, though, as *Goryeosa Jeollyo* (*Essentials of Goryeo History*) recounts: "General Kim Jin debauched himself with *soju* and failed to carry out his duties, gathering courtesans and the commanders beneath him to drink *soju*, night and day, so the soldiers were known as the '*soju* band.'"

Such excessive indulgence in *soju* continued into the Joseon period. *The Annals of King Seongjong* (r. 1469–1494) notes that Censor-General Jo Hyo-dong advised the king: "During the reign of King Sejong, the noble households rarely consumed *soju*, but now all consume it even at ordinary parties, causing tremendous waste. So let it please Your Majesty to forbid all such consumption." On the other hand, *soju* was used for medicinal purposes as well; *The Annals of King Danjong* (r. 1452-1455) reveals that the sickly young king was administered *soju* as a medicine. *Jibongyuseol* (*Topical Discourses of Yi Su-gwang*), published in the early 17th century, reads, "*Soju* is used as a medicine, so people did not drink a lot of it but drank from small glasses, thus leading to the custom of calling small glasses '*soju* glasses.'"

Trials of Traditional Soju

By the Joseon era, many families made alcohol at home for their own use, and various texts recorded the methods for producing distilled *soju*. Each region had its own special methods, leading to many popular *soju* varieties, such as stoneweed-flavored *gamhongno*, roasted bamboo–flavored *jungnyeokgo*, pear and ginger–flavored *iganggo*, and glutinous rice–based *samhae soju*. When the first liquor tax law was passed in 1909, Korea had practically become a protectorate of Japan. In 1916, the Japanese government-general of Korea promulgated the even stricter Liquor Tax Act, which served to erode not only home distilling but also commercial liquor production, which was driven primarily by Korean capital.

As the Japanese tightened their grip, regional production of traditional liquors collapsed and the Korean liquor industry was reorganized around Japanese capital. There were over 28,000 *soju* producers in 1916, but by 1933 that number had plummeted to 430. In 1934, the licensing system for home brewing and distilling was abolished, causing homemade liquors to disappear. As a result, the government-general's liquor tax revenue increased sharply: In 1918, the colonial government collected 12 times the amount of liquor taxes generated in 1909, and by 1933, liquor taxes accounted for 33 percent of all taxes collected in Korea. Along the way, *soju* brewed with traditional malt and distilled with Korean-style stills was gradually replaced by *soju* made with Japanese-style steamers and black yeast.

Traditionally distilled *soju* managed to survive despite various hardships, but in 1965 it faced its greatest trial. In order to boost the food supply, the Korean government enacted the Grain Management Law, which prohibited the use of grains for the manufacture of alcohol. Traditionally distilled *soju* made from rice thus became a thing of the past. In its place, a new type of *soju* emerged, which was mass produced by diluting stronger alcohol distilled from sweet potatoes, molasses, tapioca and other foodstuffs.

Manufacturers of diluted *soju* sprang up one after another in the 1960s, prompting the government to enact a restriction in 1973 that allowed only one *soju* maker per province; today, 10 such companies remain. This regulation was the decisive factor behind the creation of brands particular to each region. Diluted *soju* did not have a high-quality image, but it was inexpensive and had a unique flavor of its own. It quickly captured the hearts of consumers.

World's Most-Sold Spirit

The history of *soju* then came to be characterized by the reduction of its alcohol content. In the 1960s, when diluted *soju* first became popular, it was 30 percent alcohol by volume (ABV). In 1973, though, the ABV was reduced to 25 percent, and remained at that level for a quarter century. Then, in the late 1990s, reflecting the worldwide trend favoring lower-ABV beverages and an increasingly health-conscious society, 23 percent ABV *soju* made its debut, leading local manufacturers to introduce new products with even lower alcohol content. The ABV declined to 22 percent and then 21 percent, and in 2006, finally dipping below the previously sacrosanct 20 percent mark, *soju* with 15.5 percent ABV appeared on store shelves. It had become such a "weak drink" that traditional *soju* would have been ashamed to recognize it as even a distant cousin.

Soju with slightly higher ABV was subsequently introduced to the market to appease drinkers who prefer a higher alcohol content. Despite that, the trend for weaker *soju* is likely to continue. With its alcohol content lowered, *soju* has gained more ground among women, a development that more stylish branding has also helped with. Korea's *soju* brands originally had difficult and rather antiquated names consisting of Chinese characters, such as Jinro ("True Dew"), Gyeongwol ("Bright Moon") and Muhak ("Dancing Crane"). But in 1998, Jinro changed the name of its signature brand to the easier, native Korean version, "Chamisul." When this move proved highly successful, competitors came out with new brand names of their own like Cheoeumcheoreom ("Like the first time") and Joeun Day ("It's a good day!").

Bus ad promoting a range of *soju* with different strengths

As *soju* became entrenched as the national drink of Korea, controversy raged over the harmfulness of additives. Those who love *soju* often describe its taste as "sweet," and in fact diluted *soju* contains artificial sweeteners. Concern has been raised about the harmful side effects of artificial sweeteners, such as saccharine, aspartame and stevioside, but distillers have responded that these substances are not harmful and are used in many other products. However, the controversy over artificial sweeteners is a matter that warrants the food industry's careful attention.

After an eventful journey, diluted *soju* has found a home in Korean society. *Soju* can now be made from rice again, and legendary traditional liquors are now being revived, but this has not been enough to sway the tastes of the consumers who have come to love the cheap and flavorful diluted *soju*. According to 2011 market data published in the industry magazine *Drinks International*, Chamisul was ranked No. 1 worldwide in the spirits category, while Cheoeumcheoreom ranked third. *Soju* is now not only integral to Korean culture; it has joined the ranks of globally renowned liquors.

SOJU: THE COMFORT OF A NATION

As far as alcohol consumption goes, there seems to be little difference between different social classes in Korea today: You could say that *soju* brings the nation together. Behind this popular liquor is the optimism of city laborers during the era of industrialization, and this "*soju* spirit" developed into a distinctive after-work dinner culture in recent decades.

Soldiers of Industry and Their Soju

Korea's industrialization, which allowed the nation to transform itself from one of the world's poorest countries in the wake of the

Korean War to the eighth-largest trading power today, began in earnest in the 1970s. The leading roles were assumed by the young elite, who had overcome the economic difficulties of the postwar period and graduated from university thanks to their passion for education. But the driving force came from the ordinary young people who abandoned their hometowns and flocked to the cities in search of work. Their productive, low-cost labor was the single most important factor behind Korea's successful industrialization.

The glass of liquor they had on the way home from work soothed the tired bodies and homesick hearts of these laborers. Just as the workers of the Industrial Revolution in England enjoyed strong brandy instead of wine or beer, *soju* surpassed *makgeolli* in popularity as it stimulated the appetite and could bring on a state of intoxication after three glasses or so. Bitter, yet with a sweet aftertaste that lingered in the mouth, it was enough to ease the weariness of life and offer comfort, allowing the drinker to enjoy

intoxicated bliss for a bargain price. In "The Dawn of Labor," the poet Park No-hae sang of a spirit that "When the night shift like combat ends . . . pours cold *soju* on our stinging chests at dawn / For our love, our fury / our hope, and our solidarity that breathes and grows / within our rugged blood, sweat, and tears." Put succinctly, *soju* was perfectly suited to the demands of the times.

A Liquor of Optimism and Solidarity

Drinkers share common traits wherever you go, but if one were to describe the characteristics of Korean drinking, Koreans tend to err on the side of inebriation rather than restraint. They drink "to the finish" rather than in moderation. Curiously enough, the sentiment at the root of this embrace of inebriation is not escapism or defeatism but a dignified sense of optimism. The Korean saying "Even a rat's hole sees the sun sometimes" or the song lyrics, "Some day in life the sun will come out" embody the spirit that drove many Koreans to seek out bars. Though they might have been pushed to the brink of despair, they did not give up. Defeat is only temporary, so they waited, dreaming of the day when they would once again prevail. *Soju* was the comfort liquor that allowed those the world might consider "losers" to share moments of reassurance and pat each other on the back.

Drinking alone is quite a rare sight in Korea. Drinking customs here are very passionate, as if to prove the notion that alcohol can strengthen the collective spirit and solidarity. This is how the distinctive Korean custom of after-work get-togethers got started. Skipping out on such occasions (although it would probably be

People relaxing at cart bars after a long day of work

more appropriate to call them "group drinking sessions") tends to be perceived as a rejection of solidarity. Though, of course, all is forgotten the next day when the fuss has subsided. This seemingly unproductive and wasteful drinking culture, which sees people heading off to a second and third drinking spot at whatever hour, served to solidify the kind of corporate culture that was needed to boost productivity during the era of industrialization.

Different Workforce, Different Soju

As mentioned earlier, *soju*'s ABV has steadily declined in recent decades. The change to "mild *soju*" is often attributed to today's health-conscious attitudes, or an effort to appeal to the tastes of younger drinkers and women. The introduction of a growing

variety of *soju* cocktails with different fruit flavors is a testament to this trend.

The fundamental reason for this change, however, may lie in changes in the quality and type of labor. The physical labor of the industrial period, which generally strove toward a given goal through hard work and persistence, reached its peak when the GDP per capita hit USD 10,000. Work in the next era, the so-called information age, was increasingly perceived as a means of self-realization, not backbreaking labor in exchange for monthly wages. A belief emerged that people could select jobs based on their aptitudes, and that social standing could be decided by ability rather than age or loyalty. Against this backdrop, people could seek fulfillment through their work. On the flip side, you had to prove your ability by overcoming endless competition, and anyone who failed would immediately be replaced. Aimless pleasure or the freedom to do nothing were no longer options, and any time not occupied by work was not "free" but an opportunity to engage in self-improvement.

It was at this point that *soju* started becoming a symbol. Gradually moving away from the essence of alcohol, or as a way to get drunk, it grew to represent a notion of drink as a means to stimulate the appetite or improve relationships by promoting conversation. This is similar to how cars moved away from their essence of speed and are now seen in terms of safety and status symbols. The formality of clinking glasses in a toast does not necessarily require a drink with high alcohol content. Heavy drinking has become an obstacle in the competition we now face in our daily lives.

WELL-KNOWN VARIETIES OF SOJU

Andong Soju

The *soju* from Andong, Gyeongsangbuk-do, is a distilled liquor produced from fermented *nuruk*, steamed rice and water. It is said that Kublai Khan, grandson of Genghis Khan, created this liquor during his stay in Andong, while preparing to invade Japan. Andong was known for its good water, which no doubt contributed to the widely renowned quality of its *soju*. *Soju* was a very valuable commodity in olden times, and records show that it was used for medicinal purposes as well. Even today in the Andong area, it is used to treat injuries and various digestive problems, as well as to improve one's appetite.

Andong *soju* has a high alcohol content of 45 percent, and is aged in a storage tank for more than 100 days after fermenting for 20 days. Despite its potency, it is known for its smooth taste and rich flavor. The traditional maturation method was to store the distilled liquor for 100 days in a jar placed in an underground cave, where

the temperature was below 15 degrees Celsius. During this time, the jar would periodically be opened and the froth skimmed off the top of the brew with a soft cloth or a sieve.

In the Andong area, almost every household used to make *soju*, to serve guests and for funerals and weddings, but this practice was all but stopped during the Japanese colonial period. Only recently has *soju* worthy of its old reputation begun to be produced again using scientific methods of brewing, distillation and temperature control.

Gamhongno

Gamhongno is a purplish-pink wine from the northwestern region around Pyongyang. Its basic ingredients are rice, millet, sorghum and malt, to which herbs used in traditional medicine are added, such as perilla, longan, dried orange peel, cinnamon, dried clove buds and ginger. It is fermented, distilled three times and allowed to mature for 120 days. It has an alcohol content of 41 percent, although a new variety with only 21 percent alcohol is being developed. In *lmwonsipyukji* (*Sixteen Treatises Written in Retirement*, 1827), it is recorded that *gamhongno* is like red dew and the best of all wines. *Dongguksesigi* (*Compendium of Seasonal Customs in Korea*, 1805) also notes that *gamhongno* was one of three highly regarded wines, along with *byeokhyangju* of Pyongyang and *samhaeju* of Hanyang, today's Seoul.

Gamhongno is made by soaking millet, which accounts for 30 percent of the total ingredients, in water and then steaming it. A watery *nuruk* is obtained from the millet, to which steamed sorghum, rice and water are mixed in and allowed to ferment. After eight days, the mixture is placed in a pot still for distillation. The herbal ingredients, which are wrapped in silk, are either placed in the mixture during fermentation or are added during the distillation process. After the third distillation, the liquor is placed in a jar to mature.

The blending of the rice, millet and sorghum together with the perilla and longan extracts creates an outstanding taste and color. The overall preparation is very complicated and requires painstaking attention. The resulting drink is believed to promote healthy urination, cleanse the blood and cure frostbite and boils. *Gamhongno*'s devotees say that it doesn't cause hangovers or the "cotton mouth," headache or stomachache that commonly result from excessive drinking.

Igangju

Igangju, formerly known as *iganggo,* is a high-class distilled liquor that has been made in the Jeolla-do and Hwanghae-do provinces since the mid–Joseon Dynasty and is noted in such publications as *Dongguksesigi* and *lmwonsipyukji*. *Igang* means pear and ginger, the liquor's main ingredients. In recognition of his skill in making *igangju*, Jo Jeong-hyeong has been designated an intangible cultural heritage of Jeollabuk-do province. His recipe has been handed down in his family for six generations.

To make *igangju*, the juice of five pears is mixed with the extracts of 20 g of ginger, 3.75 g of cinnamon and 7.5 g of turmeric. The mixture is added to 18 L of 30 percent *soju*, which is then sweetened with honey. The *soju* must be the type distilled from fermented liquor, not the diluted variety, because the latter does not mix well with ginger. The ginger, cinnamon and turmeric extracts are obtained by soaking each in a 48 percent *soju* for 30 days. Everything is mixed together and then filtered. It is stored for more than a month to mature.

Ginger was grown extensively around Jeonju, Jeollabuk-do, which may be one of the reasons *igangju* developed in the region. In making *igangju* in the past, peeled pears were grated on roof tiles and filtered through a soft cloth to obtain the pear juice, which was then mixed with ginger extract and honey, added to a bottle of *soju* and placed

in boiling water. In *Joseon Jujosa* (*History of Winemaking in Joseon*), published in 1935, *igangju* is described as a sweet, pale brown alcoholic drink, mainly catering to high-class tastes.

The harmonious blending of the flavorful *soju*, spicy ginger, fragrant turmeric and cinnamon, along with the fresh taste of the pear juice, lends a subtle aroma to this lemon-yellow drink. Turmeric, used for making curry, is an ingredient in herbal medicine that treats mental and nervous conditions. Jo Jeong-hyeong says that turmeric contributes to a unique characteristic of this liquor—the lack of headache after drinking. Compared with regular *soju*, *igangju* goes down smoothly. Records have it that trade representatives from the United States drank this wine during the reign of Joseon's King Gojong (1864–1907). In addition, South Korean representatives took 200 bottles of *igangju* when they visited Pyongyang for a general assembly of the Inter-Parliamentary Union in 1991.

Munbaeju

During the Goryeo Dynasty, it was not unusual for a person to present a local specialty such as wine to the king to obtain a government appointment, and it is said that the family that first developed *munbaeju* did just that. The family kept its wine-making process secret and made the wine exclusively for the king. The recipe has been passed down to the family's current descendants, and in recent years the government designated it an important intangible cultural heritage.

Munbaeju is made by fermenting *nuruk*, millet and sorghum, distilling the mixture in a pot still and allowing the distilled liquid to mature for six months to a year. The final liquor has an alcohol content of over 40 percent. It has the flavor and fragrance of native pear blossoms, from which its name is derived, although pears are not actually used in making it. Although *munbaeju* is similar to the Chinese spirits *kaoliang* and *maotai*, it does not have the strong alcohol smell and flavor associated with these and other spirits.

Jindo Hongju

Hongju, whose name appropriately means "red alcohol," is a cherry-red firewater brewed exclusively on the island of Jindo, located just off Korea's southwest coast. The distinctive red hue to which the brew owes its name comes from the root of the gromwell plant. The gromwell, or *jicho* in Korean, is a medicinal herb that Koreans have long eaten or rubbed on their skin to treat indigestion or rashes. When *soju* made from rice and barley is passed through slices of the root, the resulting beverage turns crimson. Due to the root's use in preparing the drink, it has actually become something of a rarity. Numerous other medicinal herbs are used in the brewing process as well. Perhaps because of this, it reportedly leaves no hangover when consumed, despite being 40 percent alcohol. The gromwell root is also thought to be effective in controlling blood sugar levels and preventing obesity.

On Jindo there are about 20 craftsmen who brew the drink, which has been designated Jeollanam-do Intangible Cultural Heritage No. 26. Despite its current home in the southwest of Korea, *hongju* production began in the northern regions of the Korean peninsula during the Goryeo Dynasty, when *soju* brewing techniques were introduced. How it was introduced to Jindo is something of a mystery, although some theorize it was brought there by scholar officials exiled to the island from the capital. At any rate, production of the tipple spread to private homes sometime during the Joseon Dynasty.

Jindo *hongju* was presented during the 2010 Korean Traditional Food Night in Dalian, China.

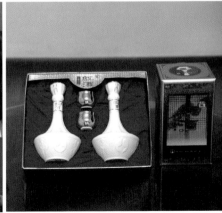

Savory Foods That Accompany Soju, and Other Korean Pub Grub

Koreans rarely drink alcohol without food. Even in the Joseon Dynasty, when people dropped by the local tavern for a quick drink they would usually be offered some free snacks. Hard liquor such as *soju* called for generous servings of food as an accompaniment; today, it is seldom consumed without side dishes, called *anju*. The Korean notion of *anju* may have no exact equivalent in the West, where people do not always seek out food to have with their drinks. While "munchies," "snacks" and "side dishes" are general English-language equivalents for *anju*, the nuances are different. *Anju* is not meant to be a full meal, but it doesn't necessarily refer to light snacks. It could be said that *anju* is meant to enhance the flavor of alcohol rather than to simply satisfy an empty stomach. At the same time, many people will have their fill of *anju* along with drinks so they won't need a proper meal afterward.

Dry Anju, Wet Anju

For many Koreans, the sight of tasty food on the table can trigger a hankering for *soju*—when certain fish is in season, for instance, this provides the perfect pretext to go for a drink after work. The selection of *anju* that complements *soju* is practically endless.

Typical "dry" *anju* dishes include a wide range of dried fish and seafood, such as squid, filefish and pollack, as well as various nuts. There is also a long list of "wet" *anju* choices, including *jjigae* (stew), *jjim* (steamed dishes), *jeongol* (stew cooked at the table) and tofu dishes. When it comes to *soju*, most Koreans favor wet dishes.

Suyuk (boiled beef or pork) is one of the most popular wet dishes enjoyed with *soju*. Boiled meat is usually served to guests at special festive occasions or funerals, but it is also a popular side dish with various alcoholic drinks. Also from the wet *anju* canon is *sulguk* (literally "alcohol soup") or *haejangguk*. These are generic terms for soups containing a larger serving of meat slices than usual. Known as "the friend of *soju*," this type of soup inspires *soju* drinkers to polish off a few bottles with ease.

(From top left) Assorted dry *anju*, *suyuk*, barbecued eel, barbecued gizzard shad, octopus soup and *haejangguk*

Seasonal Foods

Korean cuisine emphasizes the use of seasonal ingredients, and this principle applies equally to food that accompanies *soju*. For instance, particular fish dishes are highly sought after when in season. Regions and towns renowned for their local delicacies organize annual food fairs, which attract visitors from around the country to savor the area's specialties. *Soju* lovers who cannot make it to fishing areas or the countryside seek out restaurants in their vicinity that serve the regional dishes. In winter, they have *soju* with fresh pollack stew, and in spring they gather at restaurants that offer fresh flounder or webfoot octopus. In summer, croaker is the fish favored by *soju* drinkers, who will eat it raw, in a spicy broth or covered in flour and egg and pan-fried. Raw sea bass and grilled sea eel are prized summer delicacies, widely believed to improve stamina and help fight the summer heat.

Samgyeopsal, the Nation's Favorite Anju

According to a recent survey of young Korean employees, for company gatherings after work, while the drink of choice is *soju*, the most popular *anju* is *samgyeopsal*, or grilled pork belly. The unrivalled popularity of *samgyeopsal* as an accompaniment to *soju* is a very recent development. During the Goryeo Dynasty, when Buddhism was the state religion, meat consumption was prohibited for religious reasons. Even after the ban was lifted in the Confucian-oriented Joseon Dynasty, with meat in short supply overall, Koreans preferred beef over pork. Pork only became a popular choice in the 1970s when the government promoted large-scale pig farming and encouraged pork production. The rapid increase in the pork supply fueled a steady rise in its consumption, and by the late 1970s grilled pork belly was all the rage. At a time when the country was striving to achieve industrialization, the cheaper pork meat was a source of nutrition and an ideal accompaniment for hard liquor.

The same survey revealed that other popular *anju* choices are sliced raw fish, grilled beef, grilled marinated pork ribs, *jokbal* (pork hocks), pork bone stew with potatoes and grilled beef intestines. Of course, this is far from being an exhaustive list of the dishes enjoyed with *soju*. Seasoned raw beef, *jokpyeon* (beef gelatin), dried fish roe, grilled chicken giblets, *duruchigi* (spicy stir-fried vegetables and meat) and shellfish soup—all of these and more are staples with a glass or two of *soju*.

Anju for Other Drinks

Many other alcoholic drinks have a perfect match in the world of *anju* as well. *Makgeolli* is most often paired with *jeon*, or pan-fried foods. Perhaps the most common form of *jeon* is the *pajeon*, or green onion pancake, but other popular *jeon* include the *haemuljeon*, or seafood pancake; *kimchijeon*, or kimchi pancake; and *gamjajeon*, or potato pancake. It's said that rainy days in particular are a good time to enjoy *makgeolli* and *jeon*.

Another kind of fried pancake commonly enjoyed with *makgeolli* is the *bindaetteok*, or mung bean pancake. Once nicknamed *binjatteok* (literally "poor man's cake"), it is closely associated with the working class. Some drinkers enjoy their *makgeolli* with a plate of *hongeo samhap*, a dish of fermented skate served with slices of

Pajeon (green onion pancake) and *makgeolli*

boiled pork and kimchi. A specialty of the Korean southwest, *hongeo* has a distinctive and powerful aroma that makes it very much an acquired taste. *Dotorimuk*, an acorn jelly served with vegetables, is a bit easier for the uninitiated to enjoy. Also popular is *dubu kimchi*, which, as the name suggests, is slabs of tofu paired with kimchi.

Sampling the gamut of *anju* dishes is a good way to immerse oneself in Korean drinking culture. Anyone planning a trip to Seoul shouldn't miss the food alley (*meokja golmok*) at Gwangjang Market, near Dongdaemun Gate, where visitors can partake of the vast selection of foods that locals eat when having a drink.

Gwangjang Market

Chapter Four

TRADITIONAL LIQUORS AND WINES FROM AROUND KOREA

Korean liquor and wine are rich in the fragrance and flavors of traditional culture. The azalea wine of Myeoncheon, thick, flavorful *nongju*, the crystal-clear *soju* from Andong, *sogokju* from Hansan, smooth rice *makgeolli*—all are part of Korea's epicurean culture, but are slowly being forgotten in the bustle of modern society.

In traditional society, alcoholic drinks were made at home using seasonal grains, flowers and herbs. The tradition of making homemade brews developed during the Joseon era, when Confucian philosophy and its emphasis on ancestral worship, as well as celebrating seasonal holidays, became the dominant state ideology. In those days, there was even a saying that went "Good brews are made in reputable homes." This referred to the fact that "reputable" homes—including those of noblemen, the upper class and other influential figures—saw more visitors and would have good drinks ready for them. Also, during the farming season, these homes would prepare home brews for the farmers as a gesture of thanks. As such, alcohol was prepared for use in ancestral worship, greeting visitors and offering thanks to farmers. The drinks were quite the necessity for a household as well as being a social custom. In fact, the quality of a brew would often be a measure of a home's fortune. So each household would try to make delicious drinks using various techniques and secret recipes that would be passed on to future generations.

Now, however, each region has its own specialized tipples, often made by master brewers. Gourmands estimate that there are some 50 different traditional alcoholic drinks. We've already learned about some of these, such as *makgeolli* and the various regional varieties of *soju*, in earlier chapters. Here we'll learn about some of Korea's other handcrafted wines and spirits.

Overseas visitors try their hands at Korean traditional wine-making.

PYEONGAN-DO

GANGWON-DO

SEOUL
GYEONGGI-DO

CHUNGCHEONG-DO

GYEONGSANG-DO

JEOLLA-DO

JEJU-DO

1 Gamhongno
2 Munbaeju
3 Samhaeju
4 Pocheon Makgeolli
5 Gangnaengi Yeotsul
6 Cheongmyeongju
7 Dugyeonju
8 Gugijaju
9 Baegilju
10 Insamju
11 Sogokju
12 Songsunju
13 Igangju
14 Hongju
15 Andong Soju
16 Gyodong Beopju
17 Geumjeongsanseong
   Makgeolli
18 Omegisul
19 Gosorisul

SEOUL SAMHAEJU

A specialty of Seoul, *samhaeju* is made from non-glutinous, whole wheat *nuruk* and water. Brewing begins on the first "monkey day" of the first lunar month (the monkey symbolizes good fortune), with the beverage being fermented three times in naturally low temperatures over the course of 100 days. It is the only locally made alcohol fermented in low temperatures. The resulting  liquor is clear and potent, with a long-lasting aftertaste. The long period of fermentation in the cold gives the drink a rich flavor.

Produced only in small quantities, *samhaeju* is a high-value beverage that goes to market just once after it is brewed. If you don't manage to get a bottle, you must wait until the following year to try again. Originally served at the royal court of the Goryeo and Joseon dynasties, *samhaeju*'s recipe is said to have gained the royal seal of approval when Princess Bogon, the daughter of King Sunjo (r. 1800–1834) of the Joseon Dynasty, married into the noble Andong Kim family. The extent of *samhaeju*'s popularity is hinted at through royal records of the time, which stipulated that certain amounts of rice brought to Seoul were not to be used to brew the drink.

JUNGWON CHEONGMYEONGJU

Cheongmyeongju gains its name from being brewed in *Cheongmyeong*, the latter third of the second lunar month, when the weather finally begins to warm up and the skies start to clear.

The most important ingredient of *cheongmyeongju* is the superb water of the Jungwon (today's Chungju) region, which is pumped up from aquifers 200 m under the ground. These pure waters are said to be the reason behind the (reportedly) exceptionally long lifespans of the locals. Other ingredients

NURUK: THE KEY TO THE AUTHENTIC TASTE OF KOREAN BREWS

The first thing to prepare when making traditional Korean alcohol—and the ingredient that determines the success or failure of a drink—is *nuruk*, or a starter that consists of enzyme-carrying mold that has been bred in grain. *Nuruk* is made by mixing water and grains like rice or wheat to make a batter, and waiting for bacteria to form for fermentation. In the West, malt is used to make fruit-based or grain-based alcohol, but in Korea, all traditional alcohol is made with *nuruk*. In fact, *nuruk* is common in alcohol production across East Asia, though the type of *nuruk* used differs by country. For example, in Japan, rice *nuruk* is used, while in China and Korea, wheat *nuruk* is more common.

Traditional *nuruk* (referred to as *gokja* or *gukja* in Chinese characters) is made when mold, yeast, lactic acid bacteria and other microbes form naturally. This *nuruk* helps rice sweeten and ferment at the same time. When *nuruk* is fermented, the first thing to grow is lactic acid bacteria. After this, yeast forms, creating carbon dioxide and heat. The batter rises like bread and becomes warm. After a certain period, the yeast stops growing and the batter cools and stiffens. This is when mold grows. This whole process is repeated numerous times; after all the liquid evaporates with the heat, the process is complete. A well-fermented *nuruk* is then put through sterilization, deodor-

include glutinous rice and medicinal herbs, and roots such as ginseng and boxthorn.

Interestingly enough, the brewing process for *cheongmyeongju* is something of a precursor of modern brewing techniques, with bacteria or yeast being added to the *nuruk*. Well-matured *cheonmyeongju* has a distinctively fruity aroma, which comes from the fermenting wheat husk in the *nuruk*. The alcohol content is not especially high, making it perfect for more restrained drinkers. In addition, drinking moderate amounts of *cheongmyeongju* is said to improve circulation and help with neuralgia.

---

ization and bleaching pro-
cesses, before being used
to make alcohol.

On the other hand, *ipguk*,
or modified *nuruk*, stem-
ming from traditional Japanese methods of brewing,
is made by growing only
certain types of microbes
by artificially inoculating
specific bacteria on sterilized cultures. Thus, it

doesn't include lactic acid bacteria or yeast. So when using *ipguk* or modified *nuruk* to make alcohol, lactic acid bacteria and culture yeast needs to be included separately.

As modified *nuruk* became popular during the Japanese colonial period in Korea, traditional *nuruk* started to disappear. However, some brewmasters continue today with the time-honored custom of making traditional *nuruk*. Alcohol made with traditional *nuruk* boasts a much more flavorful aroma and taste compared to alcohol made with modified *nuruk*.

Gyeryong Baegilju

Baegilju is a popular traditional wine in the Chungcheong-do, Jeolla-do and Gyeongsang-do provinces in southern Korea. It is also known as *sinseonju*, "wine of the immortals." The recipe for this wine was supposedly given to Yi Chungjeonggong, a high-ranking civil servant, by King Injo (r. 1623–1649), the 16th king of the Joseon Dynasty. Having been handed down through the Yi family for 14 generations, the recipe is today kept alive by Ji Bok-nam, whose husband, Yi Hoeng, is a descendant of Yi Chungjeonggong. Ji was designated a holder of an intangible cultural heritage by the Chungcheongnam-do provincial government and a brewing expert by the Ministry of Agriculture and Forestry.

The main ingredients of *baegilju* are glutinous rice and whole wheat, to which other minor ingredients are added, including chrysanthemum, Schisandra chinensis fruit, azalea flower, safflower and pine needles. These plants are cultivated by the wine maker herself, and the chrysanthemum is a native variety. The most important ingredient for making good wine is top-quality water. Ji uses only water drawn from a well on a particular hill in Gongjeong-dong, Gongju, which never runs dry even in times of drought. The water is of the perfect quality to make *baegilju*.

Baegilju has an alcohol content of 16 to 18 percent, and is well known for its smooth taste and aroma. In the old days, the first lunar month was considered the best time to brew *baegilju*, but with temperatures now far easier to control, it is brewed year-round. The fermented substance is distilled to obtain a 40-proof spirit.

Myeoncheon Dugyeonju

According to *lmwonsipyukji*, wines made with flower petals and other aromatic materials are listed as aromatic wines. To create this distinctive aroma, medicinal or other herbs are added to grain wine, creating such delicacies as pine shoot wine, pine leaf wine or ginseng wine. These drinks have been mentioned in written records since the Goryeo Dynasty.

During the Goryeo Dynasty, the most famous such tipple was flower wine, including chrysanthemum wine, peach flower wine, pine pollen wine and azalea wine. Of them, azalea wine, *dugyeonju*, is the most frequently mentioned.

Dugyeonju made in Myeoncheon, Chungcheongnam-do, is the most famous of all. Its base is made by adding boiled water to washed, powdered rice. The mixture is stirred well and left overnight to cool. Wheat flour and powdered *nuruk*—sifted in advance through a silk-thread sieve and placed outside to gather dew—are blended into the mixture. Azalea flowers, their stamens removed, are added to the concoction along with either glutinous or steamed nonglutinous rice. The flower petals and the rice are not

mixed together, but alternated in layers. Another method is to place a silk purse of dried azaleas in the wine when it is fermented for over a month. The wine-making process takes more than 100 days, with the azaleas giving the wine a lovely color and aroma. The alcohol content in azalea wine is over 18 percent.

In Myeoncheon, *dugyeonju* plays a central role in a local legend involving Bok Ji-gyeom, a prominent local figure known for his role in the founding of the Goryeo Dynasty. Once Bok fell ill, no medicine could help him. His daughter, Yang-ran, climbed Mt. Amisan to offer a l00-day prayer for her father. On the last day of her prayer, a god appeared in her dream and told her to make wine with well water, azalea flowers and sticky rice, and after 100 days she should give it to her father regularly for an extended period. She did this and Bok recovered. The god also told her to plant a gingko tree, which, along with the famous well, has survived to the present day.

Cheongyang Gugijaju

Once upon a time, according to a legend, a passerby saw a young woman whipping a white-haired man who looked more than 80 years old. When the stranger asked the woman why she was beating the man, she said the old man was her son, but he looked much older because he had not drunk *gugijaju*, a liquor made with wolf-berries. She was 395 years old. The passerby returned home, made the wolfberry wine and drank it himself. Over 300 years elapsed, and he didn't age a day.

The ingredients of this wine are *nuruk*, rice, malt, water and wolfberry plant including its berries, roots and leaves. The mixture is stored in a cave for five to seven days for fermentation. When the wine is ready, it is filtered through a bamboo strainer. *Gugijaju* is a clear, yellowish brown, with a sticky texture, rich aroma and refreshing taste. The alcohol content is about 16 percent, which makes it difficult to store for longer periods. *Gugijaju* keeps for about a month at 15 degrees Celsius, and longer in a cave or, more likely these days, a refrigerator. It maintains its original flavor better if stored in a clay jar, and tastes smoother if warmed before serving.

Ancient documents proclaim that wolfberries are good for you regardless of your constitution, while legends tout them as a miracle drug for longevity. *Donguibogam* (*Exemplar of Korean Medicine*, 1613), states that wolfberry has no toxicity and is good for strengthening bones and muscles as well as relieving fatigue and increasing energy. Today, it is widely held to be an effective tonic for stomach, liver and heart troubles. Wolfberry also contains rutin, which strengthens capillaries, and betaine, which normalizes liver functions, as well as essential fatty and amino acids, vitamin B and vitamin C.

Hansan Sogokju

Sogokju is believed to have been produced in Hansan, Chungcheongnam-do, since the Baekje period. Regarded by connoisseurs as a true classic of Korean wine, *sogokju* begins life as water drawn from a well in Poam-ri, Hansan-myeon. Only a small amount of *nuruk* is added to a mixture of glutinous rice and nonglutinous rice to make the wine, hence the name *sogokju*,

meaning "small *nuruk* wine." Some brewers use malt and others add ginger, wild chrysanthemums and peppers. There are two types of *sogokju*: One takes seven to eight days to prepare and can be made anytime throughout the year, whereas the other variety is begun in February and completed in May or June.

This is a clear wine with a clean taste. It is also called the "sitters' wine" because once upon a time, a scholar traveling to Seoul to sit a national examination for coveted government positions stopped at a tavern in Hansan for a drink. While there, he enjoyed the *sogokju* so much that he missed the exam altogether. Another tale tells of a thief who in the midst of a burglary stopped to taste some *sogokju*. So taken was he with the tipple that he kept on drinking, and drinking, until he was finally caught just sitting on the floor. Yet another tale recounts the story of a guest who so liked the *sogokju* his host served, he couldn't bring himself to leave. So there he remained, sitting down.

Sogokju has an alcohol content of 15 to 16 percent. The proportion of rice, *nuruk* and wheat flour is 10:1:1. The rice is washed, ground and cooked into porridge and fermented for seven days at a low temperature to make the *nuruk*. Then rice, twice the amount of the *nuruk*, is either steamed or cooked into porridge and added to the *nuruk*. This mixture is then allowed to ferment for about three weeks at a low temperature to produce a potent potable that is light and sweet, with the fragrance of wild chrysanthemum.

Geumsan Insamju

The *insamju* (ginseng wine) native to Geumsan, along with information about its brewing method and beneficial effects, are mentioned frequently in publications from the Joseon Dynasty, notably *lmwonsipyukji* and *Bencao Gangmu* (*Encyclopedia of Herbs*). Geumsan has long been known for its superior ginseng, boasting firm flesh and high saponin content. (Saponin is the primary substance responsible for ginseng's medicinal benefits.)

Korean ginseng has been acclaimed as a multipurpose remedy for hundreds of years, with science indicating its efficacy in the treatment of some health ailments in more recent times. Ginseng can reportedly help relieve stress, fatigue and depression, and is also thought to be effective in treating heart disease, high blood pressure, hardening of the arteries, anemia, diabetes and ulcers. The plant can help reduce skin dryness, with more recent medical reports suggesting that it may even help prevent cancer.

Many ancient records indicate that ginseng wine was first developed during the Baekje period (18 B.C.–A.D. 660). Geumsan ginseng wine is made using a unique method. *Nuruk* is first made by mixing wheat with ginseng, and then tiny ginseng roots, rice and

water are added to it to make the wine's base. This concoction is then fermented with a mixture of steamed rice, ginseng roots, pine needles and mugwort. It takes about 10 days to make the base, followed by 60 days to ferment it and 30 days for it to age. Thus, the whole process takes about 100 days, with the brew becoming more flavorful the longer it is left to mature. Very little wastage occurs thanks to the robust production process, itself a result of the ginseng *nuruk*, which is ideal for the proliferation of the essential microbes.

The wine has a unique flavor that comes from the blending of pine needles, mugwort and ginseng. The ginseng wine of Geumsan is completely different from the liqueur-type drink that is made by immersing ginseng in alcohol. Having not undergone the fermentation process, the latter is visually appealing but lacks depth.

GIMJE SONGSUNJU

Koreans have long used all parts of the pine tree to brew alcohol. *Songsunju*, a specialty of the province of Jeollabuk-do, is brewed from the needles and young pine cones of the pine tree. This gives the brew a unique fragrance that's likely to intoxicate you the moment you open the bottle. A medicinal wine, *songsunju* won't leave you with a nasty headache and is effective in treating intestinal disorders and neuralgia.

The brewing of *songsunju* goes back to at least the 16th century. Kim Taek, a member of the Gyeongju Kim family, was suffering from intestinal disorders and neuralgia. His wife went to a Buddhist temple in the mountains and learned from a nun how to brew *songsunju*, which cured her husband. The Gyeongju Kim family has been brewing the concoction ever since, and currently does so under the skilled eye of Kim Bok-sun of Gimje.

The brewing process is relatively strict. Because pine cones grow quickly, you need to pick them at just the right time, and the production requires a lot of rice and physical labor. Among connoisseurs, however, *songsunju* is among the best loved of the home brews thanks to its mysterious and distinctly Korean aroma.

GYEONGJU GYODONG BEOPJU

Brewed since the Goryeo Dynasty, *beopju* means, literally, "law wine," indicating that it has long been brewed in accordance with strict guidelines. "*Beop*" can also mean the Buddhist dharma, leading some to suggest that it may once have been brewed at Buddhist temples. Served to government officials and visiting envoys during the Joseon Dynasty, *beopju* is now a government-designated cultural property.

For the last 300 years or so, *beopju* has been brewed by the Gyeongju Choe family. Choe Guk-jun, the first in the family to brew the wine, was in charge of the food served at the royal court during the reign of King Sukjong.

Made mostly from glutinous rice and water taken from a well at the Choe family residence in Gyeongju, the drink is usually brewed for about 100 days. To get its fullest flavor, however, *beopju* should be aged for at least a year. With an alcoholic content of about 15 percent, this pure grain alcohol has a sweet and slightly sour taste.

Two Brewmasters Excelling at Their Craft

The Venerable Master Brewer of Songwha Baegilju

A Buddhist might not strike you as a likely candidate to be a master brewer, but the Ven. Byeogam, the abbot of Suwangsa Temple in Wanju, has been brewing the temple's famous Songwha baegilju for close to 50 years now. Korea's first government-designated master of Korean food, Ven. Byeogam—born Cho Young-gui—became a monk at age 12 and began brewing at age 15.

Songhwa *baegilju*'s history goes back to the Silla period, but the version brewed at Suwangsa goes back to 1602, when the great monk Jinmuk crafted a recipe to help him overcome the mountain sickness at the temple, which sits 800 meters from ground level, perced on the cliffs of Mt. Moaksan.

Ven. Byeogam actually brews two kinds of liquor: Songhwa *baegilju* and Songjuk *ogokju*. Songhwa *baegilju* is made from a mixture of glutinous and nonglutinous rice, which is then mixed with pine needles and the fruits of Cornus officinalis (a species of dogwood) and Maximowiczia chinensis (five flavor berry), as well as honey. It is then fermented for 100 days, although the highest-quality product is left to age for three years in oak barrels. Songjuk *ogokju*, meanwhile, is made from glutinous rice and five kinds of grains, which is mixed with *nuruk*, pine needles, bamboo leaves, chrysanthemum, and again, the fruits of Cornus officinalis and Maximowiczia chinensis. This mixture is then left on a heated Korean floor for seven days before spending two weeks buried underground. The name of Suwangsa literally translates as "Temple of the King of Water," which should give you an idea of the quality of the local springs, always the most important ingredient in traditional alcohol.

The First Lady of Hansan Sogokju

Designated a master of traditional food by the Korean government, Woo Hee-yeol learned the brewing process from her mother-in-law, who herself was a master brewer. With Woo's son now involved in the craft, three generations have been brewing the beverage under the label of Hansan Sogokju Co.

Woo first learned the art of brewing at age 27 when she moved to Seocheon from her hometown of Buyeo after getting married. Her own family

had brewed liquor, but *sogokju*—with its strict brewing requirements that require the utmost attention and effort—was not easy to learn. To produce the best product, she uses ingredients she either cultivates herself or has cultivated under contract.

In recent years, *sogokju* has grown increasingly popular. Woo's company even delivered 4,000 sets of the liquor to Cheong Wa Dae, Korea's presidential mansion. There are currently about 200 households in Seocheon's Hansan district making the beverage.

Chapter Five

KOREAN DRINKING CULTURE

Drinking culture in Korea has much to do with the free and lively temperament of its people. Koreans have intense feelings and high spirits, and love to enjoy themselves. The Korean traditions of hospitality and sharing a tipple to deepen relationships can, in many social settings, lead to behavior that non-Koreans could find questionable. For example, following the traditional family rites to honor their ancestors, senior relatives will invariably pass a glass of the liquor used in the rites to their underage nephews. Also, it is not unusual to see amateur athletes meet up for a morning training session in their neighborhood and follow this with breakfast accompanied by some type of alcoholic drink. Though incidents such as this might bewilder some foreigners, in Korea, drinking together is considered key in forming and cementing ties between family members and friends alike.

In the United States, liquor licensing regulations in the states of

California (1999) and New York (2002) have recognized *soju* as an aspect of traditional Korean cuisine by allowing it to be sold even in restaurants that are not licensed to sell distilled spirits. The U.S. regulations reflect an acknowledgement of the Korean custom of drinking *soju* with such dishes as *bulgogi* (grilled marinated beef) and *samgyeopsal* (grilled pork belly), among others.

WHY DO KOREANS DRINK AND HOW MUCH?

According to a 2013 survey conducted by the Korea Alcohol and Liquor Industry Association, a large majority of Korean people (71.8 percent) regard drinking as a necessary element of social life in Korea, with 65.8 percent considering it particularly significant for men.

Until as recently as 50 years ago, *makgeolli* was the most common drink in Korea's agriculture-based society. It was often served to farmers in the field as its mild alcohol content of around 6 percent was thought to boost productivity. The belief that alcohol can improve labor productivity persisted in the era of industrialization when *soju* became the drink of choice. In 2012 alone, the per capita (over 15 years of age) *soju* consumption reached 31 L in Korea, equivalent to a whopping 88.4 bottles per person. If 80 percent of drinkers are considered moderate social drinkers, the volume consumed by the remaining 20 percent would be significantly larger.

When asked why they drink, most Koreans cited socialization and stress relief. Only 3 percent of respondents said they drink simply to get intoxicated.

Farmers are eating a meal served with *makgeolli* during a break.

(Left) A consumer in the supermarket is picking *soju*. (Right) Somaek Tower makes drinking *somaek*, mix of *soju* and beer, convenient.

Soju Cocktails

Regular *soju*, which is sold in a green 360 mL bottle, has an alcohol content of 19 percent. The colorless transparent liquor is conventionally served in a small 50 mL glass. A full glass of *soju* is often consumed in a single shot, especially the first glass.

A recent trend to emerge with *soju* is *somaek* (*soju* mixed with *maekju*, or beer), which Koreans refer to as a "bomb drink." A foreigner traveling in Korea and socializing with the locals is likely to be bombarded with such cocktails, which have been a hallmark of Korean drinking culture. Before *somaek*, the most common drink of this kind was a mixture of whiskey and beer, which of course has a much higher alcohol content. But despite its relative mildness, a few *somaek* drinks, one after another, can easily knock out an unseasoned drinker.

Statistics indicate that one in four drinkers in Korea drinks to excess at least once a week, while 5 percent drink heavily on a daily basis. In general, researchers find that Korea's culture of binge drinking is closely associated with the elevated stress levels inherent in today's highly industrialized and urbanized society. Of course, the past few decades of rapid economic transformation in Korea have significantly raised stress levels, but heavy drinking has a much longer history in this country.

Coercive Drinking or Group Camaraderie?

In a 2007 survey of 2,000 Koreans aged between 15 and 64 and living in different cities and towns across the country, the Korean Drinking Culture Research Center found that 57 percent of respondents had experienced peer pressure to drink alcohol during company dinners. Managers regularly organize after-work dinners with the aim of improving workplace morale, enhancing teamwork and loyalty and encouraging communication among colleagues. Typically, *soju* is readily available on these occasions.

Another conventional practice during company get-togethers is to pass your glass to one of your colleagues. If you receive a glass full of liquor, you are expected to drink it in one continuous sip and

A local health department has made and distributed "Sobriety Cards" for people to use when they do not want to drink at a get-together.

오늘은 금주하는 날!

return a full glass to the same person; to do otherwise may cause offense. In this fashion, drinks continue to be passed around, back and forth, until everyone gets drunk.

Whether meeting for work or social purposes, more than half of economically active Koreans say they have taken part in multiple rounds of drinking on a single night. Some 55 percent of men and 35 percent of women said they have been part of drinking parties involving more than two rounds on a single evening, which suggests a general tendency for excessive drinking.

In recent years, however, there has been a strong push to reduce the excessive drinking that has characterized company get-togethers. Both government authorities and business executives have come to realize that such drinking can have an adverse effect on worker—and by extension, company—productivity. Some of Korea's largest corporations have issued guidelines cautioning managers against holding drinking parties, encouraging them to arrange dinners or other non-alcohol-related events instead. Younger Koreans, too, are not only increasingly health-conscious, but also less concerned about group identity. They prefer a healthier, more fulfilling work environment, a trend that works against the heavy group drinking of the past.

PUNGNYU AND THE ART OF KOREAN DRINKING

While no precise records exist about when alcohol was first consumed or arrived on the peninsula, Chinese historical documents tell of the Korean people enjoying booze well before the Three Kingdoms Period. Alcohol was an essential part of life, consumed during rites honoring the heavens, when planting or harvesting was completed or when families celebrated special occasions. They drank, they sang and they danced. This was true throughout the Korean peninsula, in the north and south.

Historical records indicate that, at gatherings, the people in the northern part of Korea preferred to drink first, then reveled in singing and dancing. In the south, singing and dancing were said to precede drinking. Whether this latter order was actually followed is a moot point, but contemporary evidence would suggest that drinking is an excellent preparation for singing and dancing. It seems safe to assume that ancient Koreans also drank to enjoy themselves more.

Certainly the origins of Korean literature, music and dance, indeed all art forms, shared a common thread related to the consumption of alcohol. Wine figured prominently in the "Hallim Byeolgok" ("Song of Confucian Scholars"), a late Goryeo (1216) poem telling of the escapades of gentlemen scholars affiliated with the Hallim, an academy of letters. A variety of wines are mentioned: "golden" wine, pine nut wine, "sweet" wine, wine made from water filtered though bamboo leaves, pear blossom wine, wine made of the bark of roots and so on. The poem also chronicles gentlemen filling elegant cups and drinking in turn according to their age.

Lee Gyu-bo (1168–1241), a renowned Goryeo poet and contemporary of these gentlemen, was fond of drinking. He loved poetry, the *geomungo* (six-string zither) and wine so much that he, and others, called himself "Mr. Three Pleasures." Poetry, music and wine were all temptations and means of expression for Lee.

Koreans often talk about *pungnyu* when discussing the "art" of drinking. What is *pungnyu*? There isn't enough space here for a detailed explanation, but in short, *pungnyu* can be likened to the feeling of fresh wind and clear water.

In "The Fishermen's Son," an anonymous Goryeo Dynasty poet writes a line that offers some insight into the meaning of *pungnyu*: "As far as one can see, the mountain is illuminated by moonbeams. So why do we need [a beautiful woman] on our boat? This is *pungnyu* enough for us." Are song, dance and women prerequisites for attaining *pungnyu*? The dictionary defines *pungnyu* as "the rejection of the common or vulgar in favor of tasteful, elegant enjoyment." Of course, song, dance and women are sure to liven up any drinking party, but we should remember the devotion of our ancestors to *pungnyu* to prevent such parties from descending into plain debauchery.

The 17th-century poet Sin Heum (1566–1628) once wrote about the delicate balancing act between good taste and vulgarity at the drinking table. A drinking party can turn into a drinking hell if human greed is allowed to take over. While entertaining a guest is acceptable, we must be careful not to let the party take an overindulgent or lustful turn, as the intersection between happiness

Gentlemen's Gathering in a Pavillion (Lee In-mun, 1820, National Museum of Korea) depicts Confucian scholars gathered to enjoy scenery while sipping liquor in a pavilion at a valley of pine trees.

and tragedy lies in the realm of human desire.

In the history of Korean literature, Jeong Cheol (1536–1593), a renowned poet of the mid–Joseon era, was probably the most prolific writer on drinking poems. If a friend had good wine at his house, Jeong went right over to enjoy it.

> *Yesterday I heard that farmer Song*
> *from over the hill had*
> *new wine*
> *I kicked the ox to its feet*
> *threw on a saddle-blanket and rode up here*
> *Boy, is your master home?*
> *Tell him Chong Ch'Ol [Jeong Choel] has come to*
> *visit.*

Sharing the pleasures of drink was part of the traditional Korean concept of *pungnyu*. Only a vulgar cad would hoard good liquor for himself at home.

> *My friend, if you have some wine at*
> *home*
> *be sure to invite me*
> *When the flowers at my house*
> *bloom*
> *I will call you*
> *Let's discuss ways of forgetting*
> *the worries of one hundred years.*

This old poem written by Kim Yuk recalls the custom of sharing a bottle of wine with a friend, while witnessing the beauty of a pear blossom or orchid. Jeong Cheol's "Jangjinjusa" ("A Time to Drink") is an excellent example of poetry singing the praises of flowers and wine.

Let's have a drink, and then another. Let there be no end to our drinking, as we pluck flowers to keep track of empty glasses.

After you die, does it matter whether your body is rolled up in a straw mat and hauled off to the grave, or whether the multitude mourns you as they follow your splendidly decorated bier?

Once you are lying in the grove of silver grass and horsetail, oaks and white poplars, who do you think will offer you a drink under the sallow sun and the wan moon, in the drizzle and the hail, when the dreary wind blows? What use will your regrets be when the gray monkey howls on your grave?

Clearly, only a true wine devotee would write in this way, and Jeong was a model of traditional *pungnyu*. He also wrote an essay titled "A Warning about Wine":

I enjoy wine for four reasons: for washing away discontents, for recreation, for the entertainment of guests and because it is difficult to refuse wine when offered. When discontent is my reason for drinking, one could say it is a matter of fate. When I drink for recreation, it is much like whistling. When I drink to entertain visitors, you could say I do it with a sincere heart. But when my mind is made up, it is better that I not be shaken by the words of others, even if wine is urged upon me.

Jeong warns of the hazards of wine at the beginning of his essay, but his conclusion is clear: He cannot give up drinking. This observation could never have been made by someone who did not understand the true nature of wine.

Wine has been central to people's lives since ancient times. It has

made humanity feel closer to its deities and individuals closer to one another. The warm feelings that bind people are not something that can be turned on and off as one pleases. No one can simply decide to stop drinking wine they have loved. Like the old proverb "a pan that heats easily cools just as easily," we must learn to drink at the knee of respected elders if we are to drink responsibly in adulthood. (In Korea, periodic ancestral memorial rites provide a natural opportunity to sample wine.) Also, we must never force wine on someone who doesn't want to drink.

Modern life is hectic, but when drinking we should remember *pungnyu* and the wisdom of our elders. We should savor the atmosphere and the taste of the drink with a relaxed and unhurried mind.

The Wine Stream at Poseokjeong Pavillion

In Gyeongju, the ancient capital of Silla, there is a vivid reminder of the Silla people's love for wine, poetry and the joys of a life of leisure and refinement. Located in a quiet bamboo grove not far from the slopes of historic Mt. Namsan is the site of Poseokjeong Pavilion, a retreat enjoyed by Silla monarchs and their courtiers. Today, the pavilion is gone, but a stone channel for floating wine cups, constructed more than 1,000 years ago, still remains. The site gets its name from the Chinese characters for abalone; the shape of the stone channel resembles the oval sea mollusk.

According to the writings of the Chinese calligrapher Wang Xi-zhi (307–365), in 354, on the third day of the third month, 42 sages gathered at the Lotus Pavilion on the northern slopes of Mt. Huijishan in the southwestern

part of what is now Zhejiang province for a celebration of poetry and wine. The sages built a twisting waterway on which they floated cups of wine, with each man racing to complete a poem before one of the cups reached his seat. Those who failed to compose a poem in time were ordered to drink three cups as a penalty. The game soon spread throughout China, with courtiers and aristocrats building similar wine streams in their gardens to enjoy the company of good friends, wine and poetry. The custom later spread to the Silla Kingdom, too.

Reenacting the tradition of floating a cup of drink on a running stream

Many of the wine streams were built in the shape of the Chinese character for country or wind, but the Poseokjeong Pavillion's wine stream was modeled after an abalone shell. The width of the stream is uneven but it measures approximately 35 centimeters across, 26 centimeters deep and 10 meters long. According to a 1991 study by the Gyeongju Cultural Research Institute, which actually recreated the game, it takes approximately 10 minutes for a cup to float along the entire stream, more than enough time to compose a simple poem.

APPENDIX

INFORMATION

Alcohol Museums

1. Jeonju Traditional Wine Museum 전주전통술박물관

Address: 71, Hanji-gil, Wansan-gu, Jeonju-si, Jeollabuk-do
Tel: +82-63-287-6305 Website: urisul.net

This museum opened in 2002 with the aim of reviving Korea's home brew traditions. In addition to displays, the museum also hosts classes and hands-on programs aimed at promoting Korea's drinking culture. In addition, it serves as a consultancy for local families who would like to learn how to brew their own tipples.

2. Baedari Korean Traditional Wine Museum 배다리술박물관

Address: 120-24, Suyeogi-gil, Deogyang-gu, Goyang-si, Gyeonggi-do
Tel: +82-31-967-8052 Website: www.baedari.kr

Located in the town of Goyang just northwest of Seoul, this museum is part of the Baedari Brewery, founded in 1916 and still going strong after five generations. Baedari is best known for producing the *makgeolli* supplied to Korea's presidential mansion during the rule of President Park Chung-hee (1961–1979). The museum holds old brewing equipment and tools, photos and other brewing-related displays.

3. Sool Gallery Sansawon 산사원

Address: 512, Hwahyeon-ri, Hwahyeon-myeon, Pocheon-si, Gyeonggi-do
Tel: +82-31-531-9300 Website: www.sansawon.co.kr

Located in Pocheon, famous for producing some of Korea's finest *makgeolli*, the Sansawon not only has lots of interesting brewing-related exhibits but also offers classes on making your own homemade liquor, including fermented fruit drinks and other seasonal specialties. The gardens are quite lovely, too.

4. Andong Soju and Traditional Food Museum 안동소주박물관

Address: 71-1, Gangnam-ro, Andong-si, Gyeongsangbuk-do
Tel: +82-54-858-4541 Website: www.andongsoju.net

Founded by master brewer Jo Ok-hwa, the Andong Soju and Traditional Food Museum teaches visitors about Andong *soju*, one of Korea's best-known folk liquors, and also the unique regional cuisine of the Andong region.

5. Liquorium 리쿼리움

Address: 12, Tapjeongan-gil, Gageum-myeon, Chungju-si, Chungcheongbuk-do
Tel: +82-43-855-7333 Website: www.liquorium.com

Chungju's Liquorium bills itself as the world's first liquor museum. Most of the place is dedicated to Western brews such as whiskey and beer, but there's a section on Korean traditional spirits as well. It also hosts educational programs for all ages.

BREWERIES

1. Sinpyeong Brewery 신평양조장

Address: 813, Sinpyeong-ro, Sinpyeong-myeon, Dangjin-si, Chungcheongnam-do
Tel: +82-41-362-6080

This historic brewery's Baengnyeon (White Lotus) Makgeolli was given an award at the 2012 Korea Liquor Contest and took bronze at the 2013 International Wine and Spirit Competition in the United Kingdom. Hands-on programs and tastings are available.

2. Daegang Brewery 대강양조장

Address: 60, Daegang-ro, Daegang-myeon, Danyang-gun, Chungcheongbuk-do
Tel: +82-43-422-0077

Famous for providing the Sobaeksan Makgeolli that appears on the table at Cheong Wa Dae dinners, this brewery lets visitors experience the brewing process and try some of the product, too.

3. Jeonju Hanok Village Brewery 한옥마을 양조장

Address: 15, Dongmun-gil, Wansan-gu, Jeonju-si, Jeollabuk-do
Tel: +82-63-287-6330

This place brews *cheongju* and *takju* based on local home brews. They also run tasting events for locals and foreigners alike.

Jeonju Hanok Village Brewery

4. Hansan Sogokju 한산소곡주

Address: 1118, Chungjeol-ro, Hansan-myeon, Seocheon-gun, Chungcheongnam-do
Tel: +82-41-951-0290

This is where *sogokju*, with its 1,500-year history as the favorite drink of the Baekje royal court, is made. There's a free museum on the grounds as well.

5. Taein Brewery 태인합동주조장

Address: 17, Changheung-2gil, Taein-myeon, Jeongeup-si, Jeollabuk-do
Tel: +82-63-534-4018

This brewery is famous for its *jungnyeokgo*, a form of *soju* that was one of the three most-prized drinks of the Joseon Dynasty, and Song Myeong-seop Makgeolli, which is made with traditional yeast. It also has hands-on programs that tie in with tours of Jeonju Hanok Village.

6. Sanmeoru Farm 산머루농원

Address: 441-25, Witbaeuni-gil, Jeokseong-myeon, Paju-si, Gyeonggi-do
Tel: +82-31-958-4558

The Paju-based winery makes wine using its own mountain grapes. You can also tour the winery, sample some of the wines or even try your hand at the wine-making process.

7. Daesan Agricultural Association 대산영농조합

Address: 283, Aewon-ro, Aewol-eup, Jeju-si, Jeju-do
Tel: +82-41-362-6080

This place makes two of Jeju-do's local specialties, *omegisul* and *gosorisul*. There are *omegitteok* and *omegisul*-making programs for both locals and foreigners.

8. HB Insamju House 정헌배 인삼주가

Address: 165-22, Bogaewonsam-ro, Anseong-si, Gyeonggi-do
Tel: +82-31-677-3363

This *insamju* brewery is run by Dr. Jeong Heon-bae, who studied globalization strategies for French wine in Paris. Since returning to Korea, he has worked to improve and globalize Korean traditional liquors.

9. Gyeongju Gyodong Beopju 경주 교동법주

Address: 19-21, Gyochonan-gil, Gyeongju-si, Gyeongsangbuk-do
Tel: +82-54-772-2051

This brewery is located just next to the Choe House, whose residents have been brewing *beopju* for three centuries. You can look around both the home and the brewery.

RESEARCH CENTERS AND EDUCATIONAL INSTITUTIONS

1. Korean Home Brew Research Center 한국가양주연구소

Address: 10-15, Bangbae-ro 6-gil, Seocho-gu, Seoul
Tel: +82-2-583-5225 Website: www.suldoc.com

This center was founded to promote home brewing in Korea through the sharing of recipes and other information, especially online. The institute offers reasonably priced online courses for the serious home brewer. It also hosts trips, seminars and other promotional events.

Korean Traditional Wine Research Institute

2. Korean Traditional Wine Research Institute 한국전통주연구소

Address: 62, Jahamun-ro, Jongno-gu, Seoul
Tel: +82-2-389-8611 Website: www.ktwine.or.kr

Run by Park Rok-dam, an authority on Korean traditional wines, the Korean Traditional Wine Research Institute conducts studies on Korean alcohol, runs classes on brewing, hosts symposiums and engages in a variety of other activities to promote local brewing culture.

The content of this book has been compiled, edited and supplemented by Robert Koehler based on the following articles published in *KOREANA* magazine:

KOREANA, Vol.10, No.4, Winter 1996
"History of Traditional Korean Alcoholic Drinks"
 by Lee Hyo-gee
"Ten Best Traditional Korean Wines" by Yu Tae-jong
"Korean Drinking Customs" by Choi Seung-beom
"Jumak: A Haven for Travelers" by bae Do-sik

KOREANA, Vol.27, No.4, Winter 2013
"A Poet's Reverie on Soju" by Lee Chang-guy
"World's Best Selling Distilled Liquor" by Ye Jong-suk
"Why Do Koreans Drink and How Much?"
 by Cho Surng-gie
"Savory Foods that Accompany Soju" by Ye Jong-suk

Chapter 2 was newly written by Robert Koehler.

PHOTOGRAPHS

CREDITS

Publisher	Kim Hyung-geun
Writer	Robert Koehler
Editor	Kim Eugene
Copy Editor	Niels Footman
Proofreader	Jaime Stief
Designer	Cynthia Fernández